W9-CBR-043

JOURNAL ME ORGANIZED

THE COMPLETE GUIDE TO PRACTICAL AND CREATIVE PLANNING

Rebecca Spooner

Get Creative 6

Get Creative 6

An Imprint of Mixed Media Resources

104 West 27th Street

New York, NY 10001

Editorial Director

Maius Minus llc

Art Director

Irene Ledwith

Designer

Alison Wilkes

Associate Editor

Jacob Seifert

Photography

Rebecca Spooner

Additional Photography

Marcus Tullis

Production

J. Arthur Media

Publisher

Caroline Kilmer

Creative Director

Diane Lamphron

Production Manager

David Joinnides

President

Art Joinnides

Chairman

Jay Stein

To HS:

Without whom this book would never have existed. Through these pages you inspired me to dig deeper and discover the creativity within me.

— It's all for you —

Copyright © 2018 by Rebecca Spooner

All rights reserved. No part of this publication may be reproduced or used in any form or by any means—graphic, electronic, or mechanical, including photocopying, recording, or information storage and retrieval systems—without permission of the publisher.

The designs in this book are intended for the personal, noncommercial use of the retail purchaser and are under federal copyright laws; they are not to be reproduced in any form for commercial use. Permission is granted to photocopy content for the personal use of the retail purchaser.

Library of Congress Cataloging-in-Publication Data

Names: Spooner, Rebecca (Homeschool blogger), author.
Title: Journal me organized : the complete guide to practical and creative
   planning / Rebecca Spooner.
Description: New York : Get Creative 6, 2018. | Includes index.
Identifiers: LCCN 2017056980 | ISBN 9781640210134 (paperback)
Subjects: LCSH: Scrapbook journaling. | Diaries (Blank-books) | Appointment
   books. | Time management. | BISAC: SELF-HELP / Creativity.
Classification: LCC PN245 .S66 2018 | DDC 745.593/8--dc23
LC record available at https://lccn.loc.gov/2017056980

Manufactured in China

3 5 7 9 10 8 6 4

First Edition

ACKNOWLEDGMENTS

The process of creating this book has been more engrossing and complex than I ever could have imagined. The natural writer in me only considered the text portion of the project; I never thought about the hours of drawing, photography, and editing that went along with it. Throughout the process of scribbling notes on scraps of paper to capture every creative impulse, and sketching late at night in the flickering light of the TV, or typing furiously on the keyboard still in my pajamas in the afternoon, there have been so many people who have nurtured the artist in me. Whether it is long conversations and letting me dream (I'm raising a giant mug of coffee to you, Sonia) or encouraging my writing and the possibilities ahead of me (that's all you, Mom and Dad), I could not have come this far without all of you. However, no one has been more instrumental in the creation of this book—taking up positions on the front lines of my writing career—than my family.

Taking care of our five kids while I stole away to Starbucks to work, making dinner, putting up with my chaos and stress, my husband, Jonathan, has been my anchor. He has supported me and encouraged me and kept me going when I felt like giving up. He fed my coffee addiction and made sure I ate breakfast. He helped me set up a photography studio that eventually took over the basement. Without his support, this book truly would not have been possible. And to my littles—Caleb, Selah, Malakai, Aliyah, and Janiah—I love each one of you so much. You are my inspiration, and I am so thankful to each and every one of you!

I am deeply indebted to my publishing team and specifically to Joan, who walked me through the process every step of the way and saw potential in me. I am grateful as well to Irene and Alison, who worked their magic with my pictures and put together a design that I couldn't have envisioned on my own. Thanks go to everyone at Get Creative 6 who helped turn my dream into a reality.

And to everyone else who is a part of my life: new friends and old, people who have prayed for me, encouraged me and helped with my kids, you know who you are. Thank you for believing in me and being a part of my journey.

CONTENTS

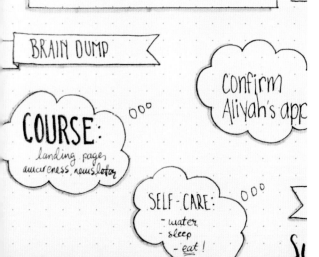

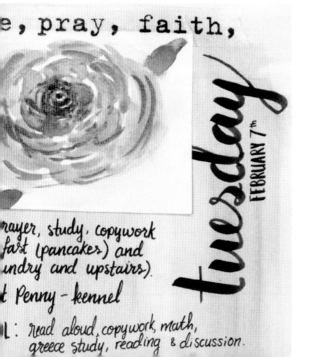

INTRODUCTION

PLANNING, WHICH CAN BE CONSIDERED A SPECIAL FORM OF journaling, is a method of mental organization that is rapidly increasing in popularity. I receive hundreds of comments from people who are discovering the freedom, efficiency, and focus that planning is giving them. Yet I receive nearly the same amount of messages from people who believe they are lacking in two areas that would prevent them from being successful at planning: creativity and attention to detail. When I began to consider creating this book, my first thought was that if I could do it, anyone could! I had never taken an art class, have very little discipline, and barely have enough time to hop in the shower. Keeping chaos under control is a challenge every day. By the time four p.m. rolls around and the demands of the dinner hour and bedtime loom before me, I can barely think! Yet despite my lack of artistic ability and time, planning has become not only a necessary part of my weekly routine, but also a welcome one. Instead of viewing it as a chore, I embrace it as time alone with my thoughts. I organize my days, weeks, and months, sometimes with broad strokes but often with detail. I smooth out the pages and begin drawing lines and doodles with my crisp black pen, and I find peace.

ACHIEVING PLANNER PEACE

This contented state of mind is often referred to as "planner peace" in planner circles. (If you aren't part of an online planning community, join one! There are literally hundreds of thousands of people forming communities with ideas and inspiration from all over the world.) Planner peace is the stage in your planning journey when you have found a system that works for you and a rhythm to your planning that is realistic and achievable. This is my goal for you. Perhaps you picked up this book because you are tired of cookie-cutter planners and calendars that don't seem to fit. Maybe you have spent hundreds of dollars on pretty little planners and failed to stick with them time and time again. Perhaps the creative side of you is drawn to the possibilities of designing your own pages. Whatever your reason for opening up these pages, inside you'll find an overview of what planning can look like, and guidance to give you the tools and confidence you need to begin. No matter who you are, no matter what your experience, you CAN do this!

USING THIS BOOK

There are really two sides to planning and there is no right or wrong way to do it. From a practical standpoint, many people choose to create their own planners because they want something that is functional, fast, and simple. Other people want to create something beautiful, an expression of their creativity, and a way to de-stress. Because these styles of planning are so different, this book has been divided into two sections. The first section walks you through everything you need to know and think about before you start planning. I'll show you how to create your own layouts in a minimalistic fashion as well as more artistic forms. We'll take a look at different daily, weekly, monthly, quarterly, and even yearly planning layouts to give you lots of ideas. We'll discuss how you can use a planner to track and manage areas of your life such as work, school, budget, meals, bucket list— really, anything you like!

The second part of this book focuses on the creative aspect of planning. I'll give you guidance and inspiration on how to decorate your pages with stickers and washi tape, flourishes and color, watercolor and doodles, and with simple hand and brush lettering. I'll take you step by step through some very simple techniques to use in your planner. These techniques require very few tools and little or no experience, so there's nothing to fear! Friend, remember that planning is your journey. Enjoy the process and experiment with many different forms until you find what brings you planner peace. Don't be surprised if you find you want to be both creative and practical.

DISCOVERING YOUR INSPIRATION, WRITING YOUR STORY

Before we get into the technical things like supplies and layouts, let's talk about your inspiration. Snag an empty notebook or a piece of paper and a pen, and make a list of what inspires you. I'm not talking about life-changing people or events, but rather simple elements in your daily life that bring you joy. It could be sounds, smells, colors, a certain temperature, the weather—anything! Some of my inspirations are fresh-cut flowers, a pumpkin-vanilla candle softly glowing on the desk, a drizzle of rain, or a crisp morning that has me pulling on a cozy sweater, a purring kitten on my lap, a hot steaming mug of yummy coffee or tea, the color white, birds

singing in the distance, some soft music playing, and a clutter-free space. Believe it or not, I even love a blank page! Just typing these things inspires me to go to this magical place, wherever it might be! I take my planner with me everywhere and have worked in it in many different places, but the more I can draw on these inspirational elements, the more creative and enjoyable the experience is.

ARTSY OR NOT

Art can be defined as "something that is created with imagination and skill and that is beautiful OR that expresses important ideas or feelings." Whether or not you plan on creating simple or intricate pages, when you create a planner full of your ideas and feelings, it is a work of art. And creating anything requires inspiration, something to spark your creativity. Your journey to planner peace may not always be easy. You'll start off excited and eager and full of inspiration and optimism, but eventually, it will begin to plateau. You will run out of time, forget to update your planner, grow weary of the type of spreads you've been doing. You'll spend time on the internet browsing through hundreds of layout ideas trying to find something that lights that spark again and works for you.

When this time comes, you'll thank me for reminding you that what you've done—and will do—is art. Light a candle or turn on some music, tidy up your space or cut some fresh flowers. Whatever your inspiration is, take a moment to experience it! It will help draw out your creativity and motivate you to keep going. Starting anything new takes time and consistency. You are creating a habit of planning that will help you be more organized, more productive, and more mindful. It does not happen overnight but it will happen if you give yourself room to try, fail, and try again.

1

GETTING STARTED

• • •

You don't need much equipment to get started with planning—just a notebook and a pen. But it's helpful to understand the different kinds of planning so you can get a feel for how you can best use and adapt this tool to your life. I'll define the two main types of planning, and provide guidance on how to decide on a format for your layouts. I'll also describe the different types of notebooks and discuss some additional supplies you may find useful. There is such an incredible variety of ideas and methods out there! This chapter will give you an overview of the different approaches, and how you can make them work for you. I can't wait to show you inside my planner!

CEREBRAL VS. CREATIVE PLANNING

There are two different approaches to planning—cerebral and creative—and, generally, every planning method fits into one of these categories. While you will likely identify with elements of both of these, it is helpful to understand the difference between the two.

Each of us has two different hemispheres of our brain: right and left. The left side of the brain is the seat of logical thinking. This side deals in facts, it thinks in chronological order and in words, and is mathematical and detailed. The right side of the brain is considered the artistic, creative side. It is the seat of the imagination and intuition, and is used for processing nonverbal cues and in thinking in images or pictures. Both sides of the brain work together and communicate with each other through bundles of nerve cells that form pathways from one side to the other. Although there's no proof that healthy individuals have a dominant side in the same way that the majority of people have a dominant hand, many people feel they are more logical than creative, or vice versa. If you normally consider yourself logical and analytical, but are drawn to the beauty of creative planning, go for it! If you are normally the creative type, but like the straightforward cerebral side, give it a try. What will work for you in the long term is what you enjoy and find useful.

While cerebral planning can be simple or detailed, creative planning is a very different process. Creative planning often involves mixed media, paint, and a more free-flowing

schedule. It's great for a week that doesn't need a lot of structure or organization. This type of planning takes a lot more time than most of the minimalistic pages or spreads, but each of the two types has its own unique benefits to the user.

You may find that you can't stand the structure and detail of a cerebral system and are looking for a way to express who you are that still helps you organize your schedule, tasks, and goals. You may find adding color and imagery helps you remember details more clearly. Or maybe you desperately need some organization and structure in your life, a way to start working toward those goals that never seem to feel any closer. If you want to create a system that can carry all the information in your life and yet is easily accessible, cerebral planning might be a better overall fit for you, especially if you are tracking a pattern or need to refer later to specific dates.

Whatever your needs are, I encourage you not to be bound to one specific method. Remind yourself that this is your planner, and there are no rules! You can try some minimalistic spreads, then play with some more artistic ones. Give yourself permission to be inspired, to try something new. You're probably going to learn a whole lot more about yourself in the process.

MY STORY

I have always been a very logical and practical person, drawn to a minimalistic, concrete planning style. My practical side tells me that this style is more realistic, that it takes less time, that plain black and white is clean and beautiful in its simplicity. However, when I've occasionally become bored with my layouts, instead of putting my planner aside (I've simply found it's too helpful to give it up), I pulled out my paint supplies to add a bit of color to my days. It's opened up the creative side of me!

THE BENEFITS OF CEREBRAL PLANNING

1. Cerebral planning is concrete. It compartmentalizes your days, weeks, and months into tasks, goals, and things you want to track in a way that is easy to identify and follow at a glance.

2. The framework cerebral planning can provide is extremely helpful in creating structure, particularly for people who are naturally more free-thinking than linear-thinking. This can help people follow through on tasks, especially complex ones.

3. Cerebral planning can help you define a problem and create a solution, or a series of steps to overcome the problem. When life feels out of control, with pressure weighing in on every side and you feel like you are constantly forgetting something, the very act of organizing those thoughts can help you gain control and reduce your stress.

TIP

Give yourself room to grow and to make mistakes and to not love everything you try. The journey to creating your perfect planner absolutely must have some mistakes. Portable computer pioneer Adam Osborne said it best: "The most valuable thing you can make is a mistake —you can't learn anything from being perfect."

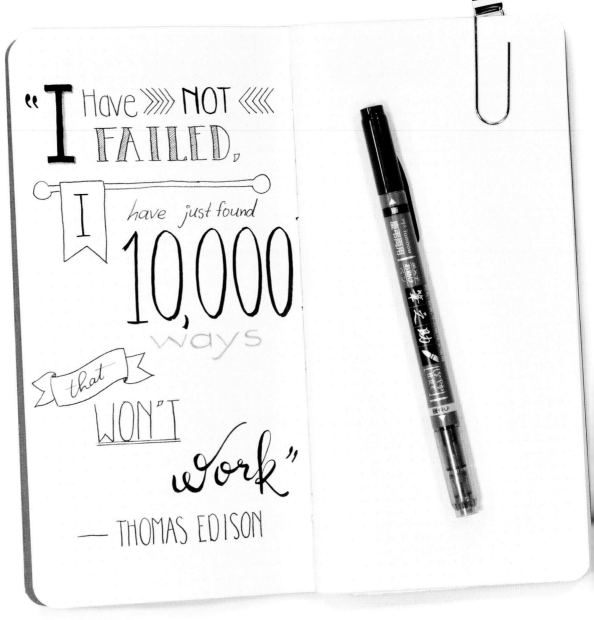

"I Have >>> NOT <<< FAILED, I have just found 10,000 ways that WON'T Work"

— THOMAS EDISON

THE BENEFITS OF CREATIVE PLANNING

1. Creative planning is an expression of who you are. It can be an abstract way of organizing your feelings, your thoughts, and unfocused ideas, all without having to verbalize them.

2. Being creative is therapeutic. It is no secret that adults have embraced coloring for a reason: creativity decreases stress. It is an outlet that literally gives you a physical way of releasing tension.

3. The more time you spend creating and mapping out and visualizing your week, the more firmly your plans are cemented in your mind. Many different studies, including one by Georg Stenberg published in the *European Journal of Psychology,* have shown that when you have both graphic and textual cues (that is, words and pictures together), the information is much easier to recall. So, for example, you will be more likely to remember that medical appointment your made for your mom because you doodled a sketch of a doctor in green pencil, her favorite color.

WHY CREATE A CUSTOM PLANNER?

Creating your customized planner has many benefits that you won't find with a pre-made template. If you think you may have trouble following through with your planner, knowing that you don't need to fill out any premade sections will be especially helpful on those days you don't feel like planning. Why did you pick up this book? Take a look at some of the benefits I have found and make a note of any that jump out at you.

Mental Benefits

As you take the time to plan your day, to lay out your jumbled thoughts and organize them on paper, something amazing happens. The simple act of writing them out helps to reinforce them in your mind. It cements the plan a little more firmly, making it easier to recall and to act. The process of prioritizing your thoughts and choosing plans that align with your values and goals will help you become more focused and intentional about your life, and thus your hours will become more efficient. You will probably find you can fit much more into a day than you could before.

Practical Benefits

As you begin to assess the areas in your life that you want to track, improve on, or eliminate, a customized planner gives you freedom and flexibility to streamline your thoughts. It can help you set realistic goals and measure your success and failures. It puts you in the position of having a vision over your life, allowing you to look at the bigger picture while reflecting on your everyday choices.

Emotional Benefits

Planning can (and should) be relaxing. It is not a chore that you are forced to do; it is a way of taking control of your life and establishing your priorities. Whether you choose to create minimalistic task lists or more artistic spreads, planning offers you a chance to take actionable steps to improve your situation and reduce your stress.

• • •
CHOOSING YOUR SUPPLIES

If the word "supplies" makes you think of a huge online shopping bill, stop right there! If there is one thing I want to impress upon you, it is this: DO NOT spend a fortune on planning supplies without knowing what to do with them, what you will like, or what kind of planning you want to do. Maybe you'll wind up using them, but you do run the risk of wasting money and putting unnecessary pressure on yourself. START SMALL!

SELECTING A NOTEBOOK

You can plan in anything: a composition notebook from the dollar store, a blank notebook from your local bookstore, a spiral notebook from the grocery store, or a fancy grid or dot grid notebook that you purchased online. One of my biggest regrets in my first year of planning was my all-or-nothing attitude. I made lots of mistakes, and I hated some of the spreads I tried. I was so unhappy with what I'd done that I'd throw that notebook away and start over. If this sounds like you, definitely begin with an inexpensive book. But try to remember, planning is not about perfection, it's about life. Life is messy, imperfect, and real. The people who are most successful with planning are the ones who embrace the wins and the fails of both life and the pen stroke.

Inexpensive Notebooks

Spiral notebooks, composition notebooks, and dollar store notebooks can all serve as a great foundation for your planning. The best thing about something that didn't cost a lot is that it somehow seems to give you permission to make mistakes. That being said,

inexpensive notebooks can be frustrating if you wish to mimic the clean look of layouts on blank or dot grid pages. The lines are often too wide, and the margin lines can interrupt the flow of your page. The pages are thin and somewhat transparent, which means that any paint or markers that you use will bleed through. If you decide to start with something inexpensive, I recommend using some simple washi tape to tape two pages together. This will give you a more substantial canvas to work on, and it doubles as a pocket to store stickers or note cards.

Quality Notebooks

If you are looking for a nicer notebook with thicker pages, you will want to look for grid, dot grid, and blank journals. These higher-end journals usually start at about $20 and can last you an entire year as your planner. The quality of these pages is much better than the inexpensive notebooks and they are all at about the same level, so the style of the pages will guide your purchase decision. You will be looking for notebooks with pages of a paper weight around 90 gsm. This weight (and heavier) means that you will have less ghosting (in which your ink creates a shadow through to the other side) and bleeding (in which your ink actually soaks through to the other side) on the next pages. The pages are usually cream-colored paper, and should be acid free. Acid-free paper lasts much longer, and it won't yellow or break down over time. Other common elements you might find in a more expensive notebook are an index, page numbers, a place for the date, or an expandable pocket in the back. These can all be helpful features when you are thinking about the layout of your planner.

Adding washi tape along the outside and bottom edges makes thin pages a little more beefy. The result doubles as a handy pocket.

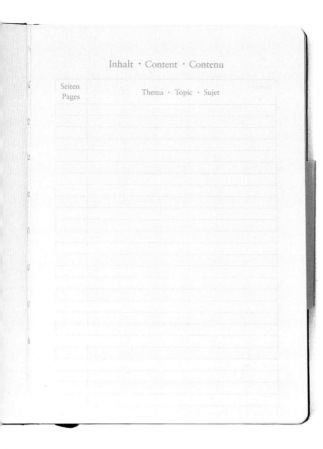

Grid, Dot Grid, and Blank

My first planner notebook was a grid and I disliked the intersecting lines. I did, however, find it helpful in the beginning stages to follow the lines and keep everything straight, including my lettering (who knew writing in a straight line could be so hard?!). But it didn't take me long to ditch that planner (remember we talked about my perfectionist tendencies?) and switch over to a dot grid, which is now my favorite. Dot grid pages have regular intervals of dots instead of lines. The dots are usually muted so that they are a light gray color. As you draw your lines over them, they tend to disappear, making the finished project look much cleaner. I find I still enjoy the structure of the dots, which help me measure out my boxes and lines. You will often see notebooks in lined versions, and these are most often selected by people who use them for journaling, though that can be a bit more challenging for creative or minimalistic planning layouts. Lastly, you will see blank journals. These are best if you are going with a creative method of planning. You can doodle, paint, sketch, or draw without the interference of lines or dots to clutter your page.

The Traveler's Notebook

This is what I use for all my regular planning. Not only is a traveler's notebook beautiful and functional, but it also offers you a ton of options on how to arrange your planner and organize your life. It can also be a money saver in the long run, especially if you choose to make your own inserts. A traveler's notebook is a piece of leather in a rectangular shape that is folded around a variety of notebooks known as inserts.

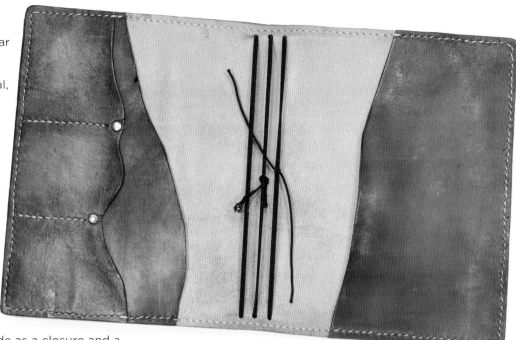

An elastic goes around the outside as a closure and a few elastics are placed vertically from the top to the bottom of the leather to secure your inserts. These can be completely customized to whatever size and use are right for you. The main draw to a traveler's notebook is that it is reusable and allows you to use a separate insert for all the different facets of your life.

TOP: The inside of the traveler's notebook showing vertical elastics to hold inserts in place. This one also has pockets. ABOVE: The closed notebook with inserts in place. LEFT: My custom cover is embossed with a feather and has a beaded tassel on the closure.

My Custom-Made Traveler's Notebook

One of the first things to consider when selecting a traveler's notebook is the size. They are generally available in three sizes, with more coming out every day. You can purchase a ready-made traveler's notebook, or design your own custom cover and have it made for you (like my feather-embossed one from Elrohir Leather or my lion one from Alt Guild on Etsy). You can purchase pieces of leather and make your own, or you can purchase make-your-own kits that come precut, and punched with everything you need to dye and finish your cover. For me, the smell of the leather, the cool feel of it in my hands, the functionality of it, and the ability to organize my life with clear notebooks for sections makes this system an essential part of my planning life. I chose the A5 version so that I can fit my notebook right inside of it. It makes it a bit bigger to carry around, but that doesn't deter me from bringing it with me to the grocery store.

Passport

This is the smallest size, originally made to hold a small notebook and a passport as well as a few cards. It is literally the size of a passport. Inserts are typically about 3.5" wide x 5.5" tall. It is often referred to as pocket or field note size as well. It is popular because it fits easily in a pocket or purse.

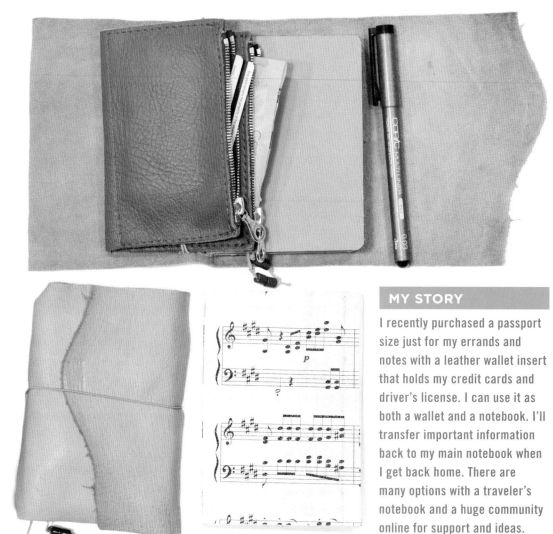

MY STORY

I recently purchased a passport size just for my errands and notes with a leather wallet insert that holds my credit cards and driver's license. I can use it as both a wallet and a notebook. I'll transfer important information back to my main notebook when I get back home. There are many options with a traveler's notebook and a huge community online for support and ideas.

Standard

This size it is a bit narrower than many others and you might also hear it referred to as Midori (a brand of traveler's notebook that comes in this size) or narrow. Inserts typically are about 4.5" wide x 8.25" long.

A5

This variety is roughly 5.83" wide x 8.27" long. A5 is a popular size because it offers more space than the standard size. An A5 fits a standard notebook such as Leuchtturm or Rhodia with room to spare for other inserts.

MY TOOLS

ONYX+BLUE

There are so many things you can try in your planner, which is why it is ideal to start small. Before you buy anything, investigate what you already have. Then, head over to your nearest stationary, art, or crafts store. Shop online if you must, but it is much easier to see and try out pens and other products in a shop than to wade through the sea of options online. Here are my most-used items; they're all you need to do 80 percent of what I do in my planner.

EVERYDAY ITEMS

Notebook

Now that you know a little bit about the different types of notebooks, what paper weight means, and the different styles and layouts, it's time to choose a notebook! Some of my favorites are Leuchtturm, Clairefontaine, and Rhodia (shown left to right on page 17). You can find them online, at stationery supply stores, and book stores.

Ruler

This little item is 100 percent necessary, unless you intend to do journaling or scripting as your main form of planning (more on that later).

Pencil and Eraser

I do most of my rough layouts and sketches in pencil and ink them in later. As a homeschool mom, I have a ton of these lying around. You don't need special sketching pencils; any old pencil will do. I use mechanical pencils because they have a really light line that is easy to erase. But, to completely erase lines, your pencil eraser won't do—you need a large, white eraser. You'll be using it a lot! The softer your eraser, the less damage it will do to your page, so look for a really gummy one.

Brush Lettering Pens

You may decide brush lettering is not for you, but as you will see in most of my planner pages, I love to add a little flair and decoration with my brush lettering pens. I have found two that I never sway from. They dry quickly, and are water resistant, so I can watercolor over the ink, they don't smear, and they are smooth and easy to write with. And the best part is that they only cost a few dollars! I use the Tombow Fudenosuke calligraphy pens. They are made in Japan, so I can't even read most of what is printed on the side, but the two I like have a blue and a dark green barrel. The blue one has a stiffer tip that is great for smaller writing and lines, and the green has a softer tip with more flexibility, great for thicker lines.

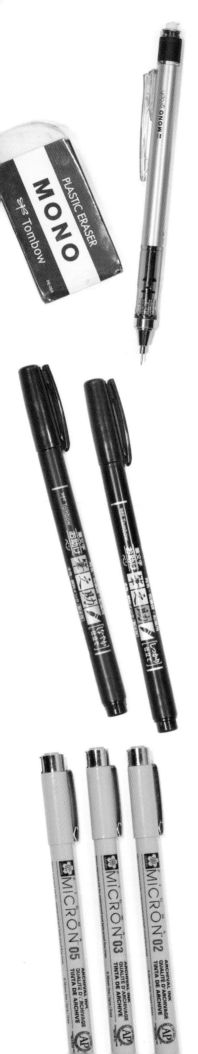

Black Felt-Tip Water-Resistant Pens

The markers I tend to stick with are Microns and Copics. Staedtler's are very common for planning, but they are not waterproof and bleed if you watercolor over them (or drip anything on them accidentally). I use my markers every single day in my planner and most of what you'll see in my planner was created with Microns and Copics. I use them under and over my watercolors, and for my doodles, writing, and outlining. I prefer to get a set with a few different tip sizes. The sizes I use most often are 005 (.20mm) to 05 (.45mm). I rarely need anything bigger or smaller for my day-to-day uses.

SPECIALTY SUPPLIES

If you find that you want to experiment with more artistic spreads, then you may want to check around your home for the following items before you make a trip to the store. These are a few other supplies I have stashed in my drawers:

- Washi tape
- Double-sided tape
- Watercolor paints
- Acrylic paint
- Paintbrushes
- Heat tool (to dry my watercolor backgrounds faster) Not at all mandatory, just nice to have. A hairdryer can work wonders, too.
- Clips (binder clips, cute clothespin clips, etc.)
- Stickers
- Watercolor pencils
- Pencil crayons
- White gel pen (to use on black cardstock)
- Sticky notes in various colors and sizes

PLANNING YOUR PLANNER

There are two ways to approach your new planner. You can begin with no plan at all, with your first pages being whatever springs to mind, and each day winging what comes next. Despite the lack of "planning," this approach offers the most flexibility. The negative side is that it can make your individual pages more difficult to find. A well-organized planner takes a little forethought before you ever put pen to page. A good way to begin is to first make a list of the different things you want to include, but don't panic if nothing comes to mind. It takes a while to fully grasp just how many parts of your life you can plan. To make this a bit easier, I have compiled a list of some of the most common things that people plan on top of their daily/weekly/monthly routines.

At a Glance...

2	DOODLE COLLECTION
3	BANNER/HEADER IDEAS
4	HAND-LETTERING COMBINATIONS
5	MY PLANNING ROUTINE
6	PLANNING SUPPLIES
7	HOLIDAY TRACKER/BIRTHDAYS
8	MY BUCKET LIST
9-11	FAMILY MEASURMENTS
12-13	SICKNESS LOG
14-15	THINGS KIDS SAY...
16-19	CHORES + CLEANING ROUTINE
20-23	HOMESCHOOL, FAMILY, PERSONAL ROUTINES
24	FAMILY FUN NIGHT IDEAS
25	INEXPENSIVE DATE NIGHT IDEAS
26-27	CONTACTS
28	BILL SCHEDULE
29	HOME RENOVATION PLAN, PROJECTS

Papier Vélin Velouté 90g/m² fabriqué en France par Clairefontaine

PLANNING

Doodles

Banners

Planning routine

Supply inventory

Tracker ideas

Planning goals

Wish list

Weekly layouts

Monthly layouts

To purchase

Quotes

Brain dump

Color chart/guide

Pen stroke guide

PARENTING

Family traditions

Christmas gifts

Kids' chore chart

Kids' routine

Asthma tracker

Friend contacts

Kids' bucket lists

Measurements

Kids' wish lists

Birthday planner

First aid supplies

Reading log

Pen pals

Things kids say

Health tracker

Diet tracker

Fingerprints

Baby names

Hospital visits

School supplies

Family goals

Family fun night ideas

Website/password tracker

"I'll find out" list

Bedroom design plans

Homework routine

Bedtime routine

SPIRITUAL

Scripture reading plan

Verses to memorize

Prayer requests

Prayer journaling

Bible verse journaling

Devotion routine

Bible studies to try

For further research

HOME LIFE

Cleaning schedule

Meal ideas

Meal planning

Replace me

Car maintenance

Recipes to try

Budget

Bills

Savings goals

Food inventory

Emergency bag

Honey do

Birthdays/anniversaries

Photo album update

Filing schedule

Free date night ideas

Dream house features

10-minute tasks

Computer maintenance

Home decorating plan

ME

Sleep tracker

Bucket list

Routine

Mail tracker

Dreams

Things that make me happy

Recharge

Contacts

Gratitude log

Undo list

Memories

Shows to watch

To learn

Books to read

Journal prompts

Favorite performers/songs

Measurements

Weight tracker

Workout routine

Once you have created your own list, give some thought to how you want to organize your planner. You may choose to have all your weekly/daily planning in the front portion of your planner while you do most of your other planning in the back half. Or perhaps you will choose to organize a month at a time and interject relative pages in between those. There are endless ways to set this up, so think about what makes the most sense to you. How does your mind work? Are you logical, organized, and linear? Or are you spontaneous and inconsistent?

It may come as a surprise, but I am naturally a spontaneous and disorganized person. I find I need the loose framework of a rough plan that also allows the freedom and flexibility to add things as they come to me throughout the week. So when I set up a new planner notebook, I start off with some of the collection pages first. I have my meal ideas, routines, cleaning chart, family fun night ideas, contacts, bill schedule, goals, etc. in the beginning of my notebook. I then begin my monthly pages, but I don't plan those out ahead of time. That way, in between months or even weeks I can add in new planning pages as I have need or am inspired to do so.

MY STORY

I love looking back at my old spreads and layouts and seeing where I started—and how far I've come. Below I've included a photo of a page where I simply made mistakes and another that I just don't really like. Don't be ashamed of your beginnings! Instead, give yourself room to learn, to grow, to improve, to experiment! Creating your own planner is about freedom, not about rules or a preconceived idea of what it should look like.

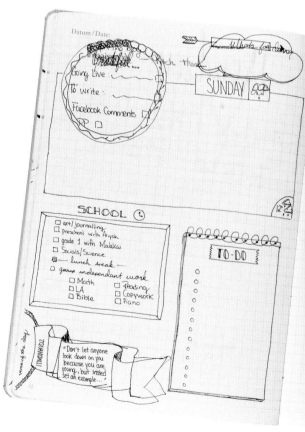

COMMON PLANNING OBSTACLES

Stick to It

The number one struggle with planning is keeping up with it. People often get discouraged when they miss a day here or there, and that can cause them to shelve the whole planner completely. If you want a more organized life, with more control over what happens in your days, you have to commit to it—and that is hard! You must form a new habit. You WILL NOT have a perfect planner, you WILL make mistakes, you WILL miss days or mess up lines or hate a page that you have done. Everyone, from great artists to little kids, has projects like that. The more realistic your expectations are, the better your overall experience will be. The key is to keep going despite any setbacks.

Forget Perfection

The next most common struggle with planning is that perfectionists (like me) want to have the best supplies, the best setup, the perfect layouts. And so they wait. They research, they pin ideas, they make lists. You are never going to learn what works best for you unless you actually begin. So if you are hesitating, grab a simple notebook off your shelf and start playing around with some different layouts. This is going to give you a better idea of what kind of planning method is going to be successful with your busy life in the long term, as well as what kind of supplies you will need.

Accept Your Gifts and Shortcomings

Another common roadblock that people encounter is that they feel they are not talented enough, organized enough, or self-disciplined enough to plan. Let me dispel that myth! Those of us who lack self-discipline and organization are the ones who need a planner most, to help focus us on a goal, to keep our vision in the forefront of our minds, and to track the things that are important to us. As Antoine de Saint Exupéry said: "A goal without a plan is just a wish." You have to plan for success! Accept the fact that this may be hard at first, that it is a new habit that you have to invest in, and that you will sometimes fail. But don't get discouraged and don't throw out your planner!

CONTINUOUS IMPROVEMENT *is better than* delayed *perfection...*
— Mark Twain —

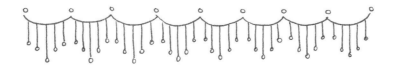

ESTABLISHING A PLANNING ROUTINE

TIP

Some people choose to use their planners as a combination of daily planning when they feel that they need it, and journaling to help them remember key events, feelings, and other things they want to recall. Often planners are a mixture of both.

I started planning because I was tired of just reacting to the unexpected events and upheavals that happen in any given week. I was looking for a way to manage my life and control what I could, while still leaving room for flexibility and spontaneity. What I learned in my first few months of planning was that the same degree of care and thought that I was putting into my actual pages was needed in the very act of planning as well. If I just left planning to chance, thinking that I'd get around to it, it almost never happened. My days would sneak on by, one after another, and by the end of the week, I would have accomplished little I had wanted, or in some cases needed, to do.

For me, the solution was establishing a planning routine. First I figured out how much time my regular daily and weekly planning was taking, how often I needed to check in, check things off, or set up new pages, etc. Once I had an idea of the time needed for each task and how often they should be done, I was able to put together a reasonable planning routine. THIS is how you make planning a way of life, a habit that you don't even have to think about. The first step is establishing a rhythm and a regular plan you can rely on when you feel lost.

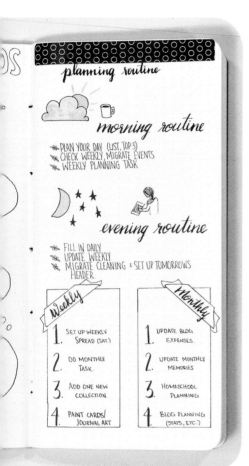

One thing that I've found helpful is to set a reminder on my phone to alert me to when it's time to plan. Think about the best time of day for you to plan. When do you feel the most creative? The most inspired? The most motivated? Is it a day of the week? A certain time of day? You'll have a much easier time developing a habit if you can comfortably fit it into a regular slot.

5 STEPS TO YOUR PLANNING ROUTINE

1. Make a list of all the different layouts, trackers, etc. that you will be doing on an ongoing basis (setting up a new month, monthly goals, memories pages, meal planning, budget tracking, habit tracking, weekly planning setup, etc.).

2. Add in a spot for topical planning. This is something you will likely be adding to in your planner very often, and setting aside a bit of time for it can help ensure you get it done.

3. Figure out the time it takes you to do each of your tasks.

4. Establish the best time in your day, as well as each week, that you can devote to planning.

5. Assign daily tasks to different time slots in your day and weekly/monthly tasks into your once-a-week planning time.

TYPES OF PLANNING

LISTING

In its simplest form, listing is just writing down tasks, projects, and events that need to be done—and yes, planning can be as simple as a collection of lists. This method of planning is great for people who want the benefits of an organized, goal-oriented life but don't want the time, detail, or commitment of a formal system. Half of the planning process is thinking about what can and should happen in upcoming days and weeks, and getting those down on paper. Because the very act of writing anything down helps fix it in your mind, listing can be a very effective way of planning that takes just minutes each day. This system also works well for people who are task-oriented and get a boost from completing things. Checking off a box or crossing out an item can be extremely satisfying and rewarding, and make you feel more in control of your everyday life.

Running List

A running list is one that is added to continuously. It's not separated by day or date, subject or theme, or priority. It's just an ongoing stream-of-consciousness document that you add to as items occur to you. It can include everything from household chores to business tasks to special events and appointments. You can create your own system for this or you can use an established system.

Autofocus

In this method, developed by Mark Forster, the user creates a gigantic list and then reads through the complete list quickly. Next, the user reads it again more slowly until he or she comes to something that can be completed that day. A dot is placed next to that item to indicate a commitment to following through with that task. Once that task is completed, it is crossed out. If it is a repeating task, it is rewritten at the end of the list. When a given task is completed, the list is reviewed again for the next optimal task. When all tasks to a certain point

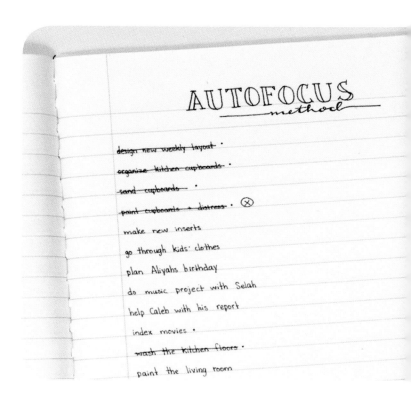

MY STORY

Autofocus is still relatively new. I love the simplicity of it! It could take you literally minutes a day and nothing will get lost as you can easily look back and work on both short-term and long-term goals as you have time. I also love how it is based on how you feel about a task rather than just priority. You can learn more at http://markforster.squarespace.com.

are completed (a running list can be pages long) an X with a circle is added to the last completed task to indicate that there is nothing active before that mark. This makes it faster to go back through a list and find the spot where your list is becomes active.

Daily List

Many people wake up and make a to-do list for themselves to visualize their day and help them manage their time. This can be as simple as writing the date and jotting down the tasks you want accomplish by the end of the day. Anything that doesn't get done is simply jotted down again the next day.

Strikethru

This slightly more complex method builds on simple list making. Users divide their notebooks into four main sections. The first section is the live list, containing items you are working on now. It usually has at least nine lines as well as an area to prioritize your list on the right-hand side. The next section is the dump, a place for brainstorming and jotting down your thoughts, conversations, and ideas onto paper so you can add them into your lists as needed. The third section is the vault, a place for lists that don't fit into a daily task set. This could be big-picture to-do lists, thematic lists (such as things I'm grateful for, or movies I want to watch), or wish lists. The last section is a calendar. You regularly refer to the dump, vault, and calendar sections to help you find items to add to your list. When migrating a task to a certain day, you can simply reference the page and task number. For example, 100.5 would be an item described on page 100, task 5. You can learn more about this system at www.striketh.ru.

BULLET JOURNALING

Developed by Ryder Carroll as an analog system in a digital world, bullet journaling was created to be a simple and effective planning tool. Over the past few years, people who have committed to this style of planning have taken the framework of the system and developed it into hybrids with sketches and doodles, detailed daily sections, and more. Many of the techniques he outlines can be adapted for use in any kind of planner. Carroll also coined his own words for some of the terms planners use, so his designations are a combination of common words and his own expressions. I'll briefly explain each of the features of the bullet journal method here, but you can watch a video and learn more at bulletjournal.com.

Index

A table of contents that makes it easy to find pages and collections you created.

Monthly Log

A monthly list of things that are happening and tasks you need to complete.

Rapid Log

This is simply the term Carroll developed for creating daily lists.

Future Log

A place for big-picture planning, upcoming events, and major or seasonal tasks, usually done six months at a time.

Daily Log

A daily list organized by symbols:

- • symbolizes a task
- º represents an event
- - indicates a note

This can be further broken down with signifiers such as:

- * marks a priority
- ! denotes an inspiration

Key

This page shows your common symbols, doodles, and signifiers and what they represent.

Collection

This simply refers to a group of related tasks, notes, or ideas put together on one or two pages so that the information is easy to find. See Chapter 3 for lots of examples of what collections can look like and how useful they are.

Threading

This is the process of organizing similar pages, ongoing collections, or tasks that relate to one another by writing alternate page numbers at the bottom of your page. If, for example, on page 32 you created a collection on home renovations, and on page 47 you created a budget for your home renovations, you could write **—> 47** on the bottom of page 32, signifying that you have more on this subject on page 47.

Migration

The process of going through your day and marking tasks that should be added to the next list or moved to the future log. This is how you figure out what is most important, prioritize your life, and weed out distractions.

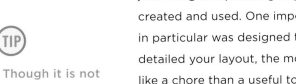

THE PLANNING PROCESS

Now that we have an overview of the meaning of the different terms used in bullet journaling and planning in general, we can focus on how each aspect can actually be created and used. One important thing to keep in mind is that the bullet journal method in particular was designed to help people plan with as little effort as possible. The more detailed your layout, the more time and effort is needed, and it can begin to feel more like a chore than a useful tool. If creating beautiful pages starts to feel like a punishment, something you dread and avoid, it might be time to go back to the basics and remember functionality. This type of planning in particular is first and foremost a productivity tool.

CREATING AN INDEX

Think of the index as the table of contents of your planner. While it is simply a list of page numbers and what is on each page, it's a very helpful tool for you to find whatever you need in your planner. Creating one will ultimately be a time-saver because you won't spend precious minutes searching for notes, lists, or collections that you created previously. Fortunately, it doesn't have to be in order, it doesn't have to be complicated, and you don't have to draw lines or boxes or a structure of any kind. You can write it as a list, or you can create your own style. Many of the notebooks I recommended come with an index already in them, making it that much simpler for you to begin this process. As much as possible, add to your index as you create new pages, which will save you time and frustration down the road.

Bullet Journal Index

This index was created in a notebook that already had a section in the front. I simply list the page number and the content of that page. Ideally, you'll set aside at least four to six pages for your index. You'll be surprised how many different types of pages you add to your BUJO (bullet journal) as you work through it. If you run out of space in your index, you can always fix that with some creative threading (see page 37) throughout your planner to lead you to related pages.

TIP

Though it is not part of the original system, many bullet journalists add a spread after their index that displays the entire year at glance. If you'd like to do this, create a mini calendar on the page for each of the 12 months of the year (starting at whatever month you started planning—you don't have wait for January!) to reference dates while you are on the go.

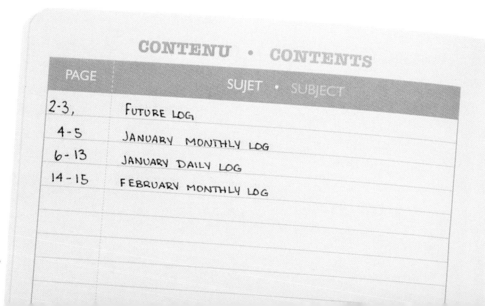

CONTENU • CONTENTS	
PAGE	SUJET • SUBJECT
2-3,	FUTURE LOG
4-5	JANUARY MONTHLY LOG
6-13	JANUARY DAILY LOG
14-15	FEBRUARY MONTHLY LOG

Custom Bullet Journal Index

This notebook had no index in the front or page numbers to reference, but I loved the cover of the book and I prefer the dot grid, so I ended up just creating my own index. While I could have easily created a simple list, I felt inspired to create something that was different from all the other indexes I had seen. It doesn't have as much space as I'd like for the page numbers, but it is minimalistic and clean.

CREATING A KEY

Many people keep their symbols basic enough that they don't need a key. Others find coding works as a time-saving shorthand. They code their notebook as much as possible, yet want their family to be able to read what they have written. Still others (like me!) use so many symbols and doodles that we can't remember what they all represent. This helpful tool can look very different depending on your needs and style. You may create a key in the front of your planner or create it on an index card or note that you tape into your journal to fold out and use as reference. Others may create bookmarks or dashboards (separators) with their key on it. However you choose to do it, this is the place to gather all the symbols you regularly use in your notebook.

Key

Many people choose to create a color key to help them organize their daily tasks. One method is to have a color for each person in your family. Writing a task or event in that color allows you to see at a glance which family member it relates to. You could also create a color for different time slots throughout the day to help you improve your time management and efficiency. Alternatively, you could use a color code for the different facets of your life. Perhaps you could have a specific color for your work, a different color for school-related tasks, or a different color for exercise. Eventually, as you become more familiar with the colors and symbols you regularly use, you will find you can quickly glance at your day and pick out the information you need.

 TIP

The key to finding "planner peace" is determining the method that speaks to you, that inspires you, that motivates you, and that doesn't overwhelm you. If on Monday you have so much happening that you need to make a simple list and lay it all out, you might focus on a typical bullet journal-style page.

I'm often asked
if there should be
six spreads after
the future log. My
answer is always the
same: Every planner
is different! How
many spreads come
after the future log
depends on whether
you do dailies or
weeklies, and if you
have any collections
or brain dumps in
the middle. Any style
of planning you use
should be easily
adaptable to your
lifestyle!

CREATING A FUTURE LOG

Once you have your index and your key, you are ready to start setting up your pages. I love that you can do this in advance so that your framework is ready for you, whether you are planning something a week or three months in advance. Set aside two pages in your notebook for your future log. On this spread you will separate your pages into three sections on each side, giving you room for six months at a glance. Once you have the foundation set, you can come back to this log and add to it whenever something comes up that isn't in the immediate future. This is a great way of planning for the big picture without taking up much time or energy.

Simple Future Log

The key to this system is follow-through, so once you create a new layout, return to your index and note your future log for those months so you can find it. You will create another future log once you come to the end of those six months. A future log is very helpful when you are doing your monthly planning, so you can flip back and see any big events, birthdays, or things you need to remember for that month. Some people prefer to set up a monthly goal page or create a quarterly planning review. Really, there are no rules. This system gives you the framework but allows lots of room to add in your own personal creativity and flair.

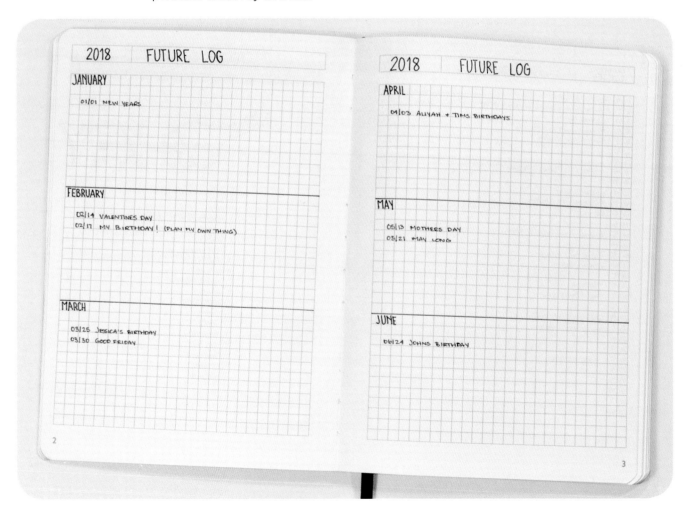

SETTING UP A MONTHLY LOG

The next spread in your bullet journal is your monthly log. Simply turn the page from your future log and use the spread that follows to lay out your month at a glance. After writing the name of the month on the top of both pages, write out each day of the month on the left page, starting with the numbered days, and in the column next to it the first letter of the day of the week. This page is where you can plan out individual events that are happening each day, or even memories of something that happened on that day that you don't want to forget. The next page will be used for listing out all the tasks that you want to complete that month.

Monthly Log

The benefit of the monthly log is its simplicity. It takes just five minutes to set up. However, if you search "bullet journal monthly" online, you are likely to come up with hundreds of variations that people use to make this unique to them and meet their needs. (Take a look at the monthly layouts beginning on page 54 for lots more ideas). The key components to planning your month are the same no matter how complex you choose to make your pages: You'll want to see everything that is happening that you need to remember that month, so you can use it for future planning, and for setting up your weekly or daily layouts.

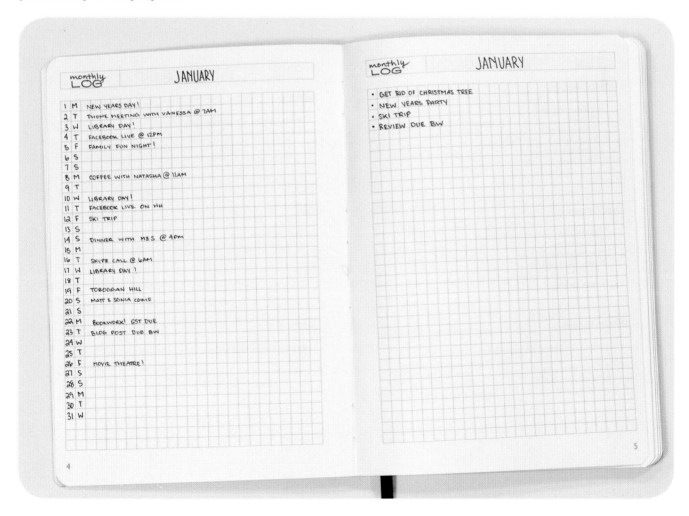

SETTING UP A DAILY LOG

This is a method of using your symbols and signifiers to quickly lay out what you need to remember each day. (In bullet journaling, this is called a rapid log.) You can plan your whole week at once, or you can do it each morning before your day begins. This is really a two-step process: first you lay out your days and then you assess how well previous layouts worked for you. At the end of the night (or end of the week depending on what works best for you), go back to the daily log and migrate tasks to plan the next week (or write it in your future log if you reschedule it for sometime down the road instead). Put an X beside items that have been completed and cross out items that you decide aren't worth your time. Without the second step, the system loses much of its effectiveness. We don't just want to plan for what is coming up; we also want to evaluate what is working to improve our current lifestyle in any way we can.

Simple List Daily Log

I like to list in the morning when I wake up. I have my planner by my bedside, so I can lie in bed to plan and assess my day. If you are testing out this planning method for the first time, start your daily layouts as simply as possible and work up to some of the more creative layouts beginning on page 44. Establish a routine, build the foundation, and then add in some of the structure or creativity you'll see later on in this book.

Daily Log with Dividers

When you are setting up a daily log that is moving from one day to the next, you may want to use dividers. These can be as simple as a line, such as what I used below, or you could do something fun like an arrow, branch, brackets, a pattern, or even colored dots or circles. A graphic element helps you separate your days and see at a glance what is happening that week. Don't be afraid to play around with different systems, tweak them, and ditch them entirely if they aren't working.

MY STORY

When I first set up my planner, I felt like a failure if I had to migrate a task or cross it out completely. I had to give myself permission to tweak my days and not feel guilty about it. I focus on what I DID do that day rather than lamenting things that didn't happen. It helps me check my expectations and become more realistic about letting go of things I don't need to do. The world will not end if I don't fold the laundry.

Collections Formats

Any collection can be a simple title with a list under it, or you could add a fun header or banner to make it stand out. I like to get a little creative on my fun collections, such as the ones that involve free time with my family. Some people like to group their collections together either in the front or end of their planner. Others prefer to just add them in throughout their days and weeks as they are inspired and use threading and indexing to easily find them. Others still use a traveler's notebook and create a separate notebook entirely for their collections. However you choose to do it, it can be a great way of organizing information for easy retrieval.

USING THREADING

Threading is an additional way of finding things in your planner. While you can always refer to your index to find your collection pages, threading can make the process that much faster. Simply refer to similar topics or related events by writing those page numbers on the bottom of your planner.

Threading a Brain Dump Collection

The collection pictured here is a brain dump—a page where I wrote down quotes and thoughts and notes from phone calls—really, whatever came to mind. I added to it and later on in my planner I created another brain dump page. This one looks a bit different but I wanted to make sure that I could find both of them, so I referenced the pages at the bottom. You can do this multiple times, with each page leading you to the next to find everything you need.

Another Option

While threading can be an effective way of finding things quickly in your planner, it is also a good gauge of things that are important to you. If you find that you are threading multiple pages about a similar topic, it might

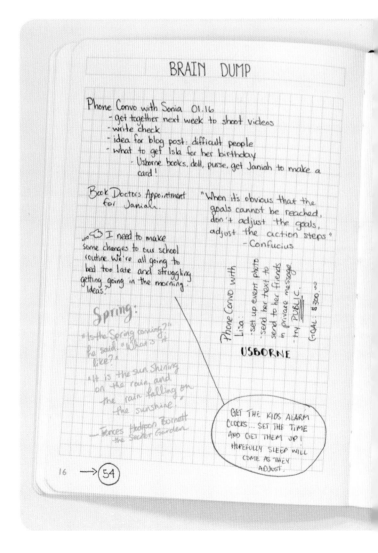

TIP

Most of the time creative planners do their planning in stages. They build the framework and the plan ahead of time and then in the evening they add in personal doodles or sketches, or paste things in that were relevant to that day.

be time to create a collection for that particular part of your life. I often do a monthly re-assessment, where I look through what I did and didn't accomplish, what I want to change in the coming month, and what collections I want to add based on what I was using the most that month, or notes that seem to be a recurring theme throughout my days and weeks.

ARTISTIC PLANNING

While the basic system of planning is very simplistic and functional, many bullet journalists and other planners have taken the basic methods and incorporated doodles, watercolors, pencils, crayons, and stickers into their pages. Any planning system or method you choose can be used in a very practical way or a very creative way depending on how you decide to implement it. Artistic planning is a purely creative type of planning that takes all the rules, methods, guides, and structure of established systems and throws them out the window. Expressive planning can have a painted background or plain one. It can be full of doodles and sketches or full of cut-outs and stickers. It can be whatever you want it to be, but generally it is full of color and expression, and a blend of an art journal with a brief overview of your day or week.

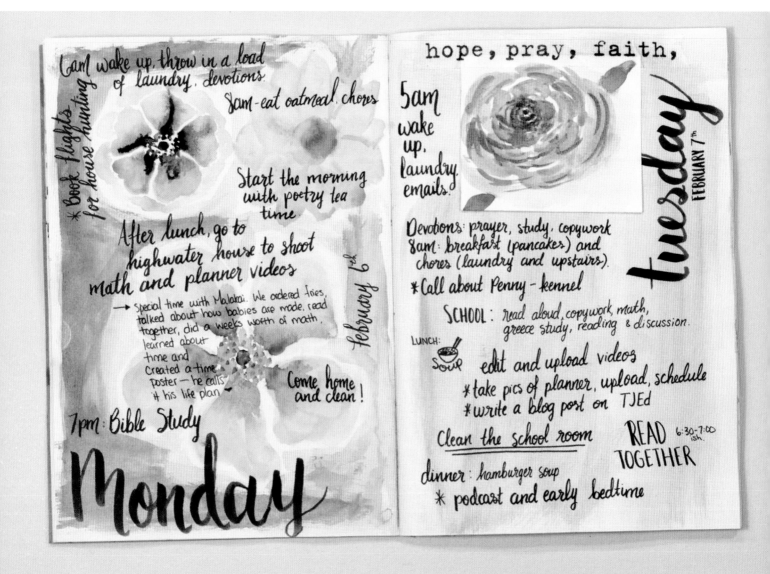

Combining Art and Planning

When you are combining art with your daily planning, you'll probably want an entire page to work on as opposed to just one section. This is where dailies work really well. Everyone's creative process is different. Some people prefer to create their backgrounds and art ahead of time and work on their planning on top of their painting or drawings. Others prefer to work on each page separately day by day, gathering inspiration from particular moments in their days to create their artwork. Find the rhythm that works best for you and run with it.

SCRIPTING

Scripting is a type of planning that is more akin to a dialogue than a list of tasks to be accomplished. This process is both creative and practical, and can help you remember your plans and be more efficient in your day-to-day life. I have found that scripting is also a gentler approach to planning. It somehow forces me to be a little more realistic, probably in part because I have less space when I am writing this way. Speaking to myself in this manner is both motivational and rational. In essence, I become my own personal life coach. I really recommend that everyone try scripting for a week in their planner to see how it works for them. It can be almost magical to see the difference between organizing your day by thought rather than tasks. The results can be dramatic. I find I have a much better follow-through rate when I script my plans rather than list them. I am more productive during my day and the process of writing out complete thoughts helps me put into things into perspective before I tackle them.

Scripting My Day

When you prepare a daily in script form, consider your day in its entirety. Often I do a watercolor wash for a background or an acrylic base to add a pop of color and some dimension to the page. Then I sit down and begin to think of my goals, tasks, events, and plans. I usually begin with my morning and the routine I'd like to follow to start my day off. I then add any tasks or events but focus more on the flow of the day rather than individual times or schedules. I talk to myself in a broad sense: "Try to wrap up around noon and make lunch" rather than: 12 p.m.—make lunch. This gives me the freedom to free-flow my day and use my planner as a guide rather than a rule book. When I am scripting, I also usually add my top three goals at the top. These are my big-picture items that help me prioritize what absolutely has to get done that day. I tend to do these types of pages the night before rather than several days in advance so I can be flexible and adapt my priorities.

LEFT: This artistic planning spread shows two days when I used the scripting technique rather than a more traditional daily log.

TIP

Perhaps on Tuesday you had an awesome day with your friends at a movie and want to doodle some of the highlights, or include your movie ticket or a picture you printed off into your spread to remember the occasion. Just like magic, you have become a creative planner for the day.

MAY 2017

	MONDAY	TUESDAY	WEDNESDAY	THURSDAY	FRIDAY	SATURDAY
	1 Selah's xray 2pm RBC	**2**	**3**	**4**	**5** Cassidy's Birthday!	**6** Mom's visit
7 nner ..sit	**8**	**9** 10:20 Selah Dentist / Mom D. Birthday	**10** Preview DUE DATE / 8pm table	**11** 1:45pm WW	**12** Usborne Enos.	**13** Kristin's Usborne 7pm
14 ..her's Day	**15** 6pm Selah's Dental Extraction	**16** Alison's Usborne Party!	**17**	**18**	**19** 9am Caleb and Aliyah Dentist	**20** Jaclyn's Usborne Party 7pm
21 ..osters	**22** May Long / Matthew & Sonia come	**23** Daxton's Birthday / Natasha's Usborne	**24**	**25**	**26**	**27** Matt & Sonias Annivers. / Lisa's Usborne
28 Jane's Usborne	**29** Amn's Usborne 7pm	**30**	**31**			

SMTWTFS
1 2 3 4 5 6
7 8 9 10 11 12 13
14 15 16 17 18 19 20
21 22 23 24 25 26 27
28 29 30 31

MAY 22 - MAY LONG

TO-DO
- Paint schoolroom ☑
- Make shelving ☑
- Make school table and bench ☑
- Organize school ☑
- Build chicken coop ☐
- Get kittens ☑
- Replace hardware ☐

GOALS
* Go through 2 boxes each week.
* Organize main floor
* 1,700 Usborne → make elite

NOTES
This month I made a goal to achieve Elite and acheived it! I finished the school room and we got a furnace put in plus a new hot water tank! Huge success!

47 9

evening
6pm bath, PJ's, story time, teeth, song 7pm bedtime.

2

BREAKING IT DOWN

•••

Everyone's planner is different, depending in part on the increments of planning that make sense for you. I'll start you off with daily planning, then weekly, and we'll work our way to big-picture planning for the year, and even goals for multiple years and special projects. I'll also cover lots of different styles of layouts, ideas of what they could include, and what they might look like. Finally, I'll share inspiration from my own planner as well as some popular spreads and planning layouts that you might want to use in your planner. I can't wait to show you what you can do!

DAILY PLANNING

While some people choose to just focus on monthly and weekly layouts, others prefer creating a page or section for each day. Daily pages allow a lot more space for planning and reflection, though they can be more time-consuming than planning your week at a glance. I've found that during especially busy or stressful times, daily spreads can help me manage my tasks (and my stress!) better.

SIMPLE DAILIES

What I love most about simple pages is that you need few supplies to complete them. While weekly spreads can be incredibly detailed, using up every square inch of space, dailies can be more open and flexible. Whether I choose to throw in a doodle, quote, sticker, or just leave some space for journaling my reflections at the end of the day, my daily spreads tend to have a lot of free space for jotting down things that interest me. For example, I have been enjoying tracking the weather on the top of my pages. I find the more information I include, the more it helps me recall what was going on at that time.

Simple Schedule
I sketched this page in pencil while I watched TV with my hubby. The next morning when I lined it in, I used my ruler and a black marker and embellished the bubbles with a bit of pink to help them pop from the page. While I tend to stick with routines as collections in my planner rather than a daily schedule, every once in a while I need a spread like this to help me visualize how much time I have in the day and what I can fit in.

Dutch Door

This popular planning method gives you the best of both worlds. By cutting off the top section of your middle two pages you can see your entire week displayed while still having space to plan and record each day. For this spread, I sketched it out first in pencil, then went over it with my Micron pen, erasing the pencil marks later. As a final touch, I added in some splashes of teal and yellow.

5   6

★ RYANS BDAY!

...day | Wednesday | thursday

TODAY'S FOCUS →

6 AM WAKE UP
DEVOTIONS
FINISH PLANNING PAGE TEXT
GET READY 8-9
MAKE THAI SALAD 9-10
CLEAN
PICTURES FOR TAGA
PICTURES FOR PTT
(COUCH, SCHOOL ROOM, OUTSIDE)

7   8   9

DRIVE HOME!
7am - 9pm

CAMP DROPOFF...

friday | Saturday | Sunday | notes

today we packed up at mom and dads and went to mom D's house. Aliyah gave her cold to Janiah and she managed to pick up a flu somewhere too. Jonathan and I went to a movie tonight and came home to a sick little girl (poor mom). Jonathan found a trailer in Sicamous

VACAY!

32°/19°

Top Three

I call this my Top Three layout because I used it to plan the top three things that were important to me that day: meals, water intake, and must-do tasks. Your top three will probably be completely different, but you can use this layout as a good example of letting go of the urge to fill in all the space. A bit of white space, large writing, and focusing in on what really matters to you are fantastic strategies for simplifying not only your planning, but your life!

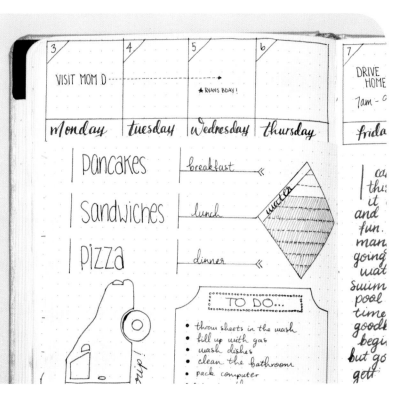

3   4   5   6   7

VISIT MOM D ------ ★ RYANS BDAY!   DRIVE HOME 7am - 0...

Monday | tuesday | Wednesday | thursday | frida...

| pancakes | breakfast «
| sandwiches | lunch   water
| pizza | dinner «

TO DO...
• throw sheets in the wash
• fill up with gas
• wash dishes
• clean the bathroom
• pack computer

ca...
thi...
it
and
fun.
man...
going
wat...
swim
pool
time
good...
begi...
but go
gott...

CREATIVE DAILY LAYOUTS

Every once in a while I switch it up so that I have space to journal my thoughts or do something fun and artistic in my daily layouts. These creative dailies generally fall into two types: journaling and artistic. While this method of planning takes more time, the investment means it also tends to represent a day in which you'll remember your plans and stay focused on your goals. The more energy you put into your plans, the more they are cemented into your thoughts.

Brain Dump Daily

This is one of my favorite layouts for a daily. I decided to track the weather with a little window into the outside (on this particular day full of sun and blue skies) with my watercolors. I also included a little flag on the bottom right for what I am grateful for that day (again that sunshine!). I incorporated a quote I love, made a very simple list of what I had going on that day, and a section for a brain dump at the bottom. I have used brain dumps in the past, usually as their own section in my planner to get my thoughts, scribbles, ideas, worries, etc. out on paper, but sometimes it's helpful to do it on a daily basis.

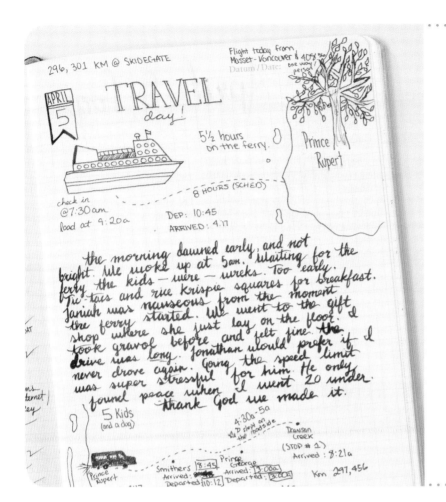

Journal Daily

Journaling dailies are different than traditional planning and come in two forms: scripting and reflection. In scripting you write out in sentence form what you want to accomplish that day, what you need to remember, etc. Reflection comes at the end of the day and describes what actually happened. If you choose to use your daily as a diary, this can be a great way of doing that with relatively little effort. When you use both scripting and reflecting, it helps you remember what happened during the day, and how well you followed through on your plans.

Creative Journaling

Another idea is to take a doodle, something that reminds you of that day or time in your life, and journal in or around that sketch. You can even do this twofold, the way I did here. I made myself a little list of things to do and goals I wanted to achieve inside my sketch in the morning, then returned in the evening to write a few reflections at the top. For me, this represents the best of both worlds—a way of planning for success but also a recap of my results.

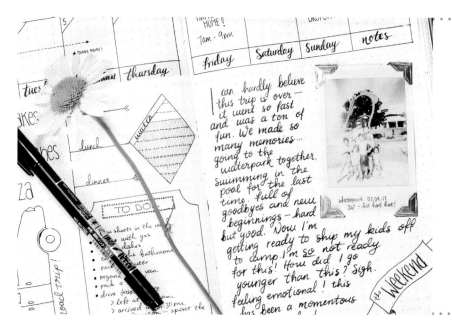

Scrapbook Journaling
The more space you have for this, the better! You can use sections of photos, collages of photos, or single photos. This technique coincides perfectly with the idea behind planning—that is, creating a visual context to improve your memory. You can washi tape your pictures in, use a double-sided adhesive, or some simple photo corners as shown here.

Watercolor
Artistic Daily
When I feel inspired to do an artistic spread, I usually begin with a theme or color combination. Here I incorporated the same color and flowers in the corners of my boxes. I kept it simple with a gratitude log and a to-do list as well as what to make for dinner. A quote in the upper right-hand corner finished it off. If you aren't familiar with watercolor, outline your design in a black waterproof marker first to have a bit more structure.

Acrylic Artistic Daily

For this layout I used a combination of a task list, a quote, journaling, and art. I thought the feather would be perfect for a little whimsy to go along with my quote for the day. I used a few different colors of acrylics together with a scraper and a paintbrush. Because acrylic dries relatively fast, it was ready for me to write my plans on top in no time.

Mixed-Media Daily

What I love about this page is that I created something fun and eclectic out of bits and pieces of things that would on their own not be beautiful or even useful. I pulled out a piece of newspaper, some cutouts, some tissue paper, some kraft paper, stickers, washi tape, and my watercolors. Before I began fastening anything in place I placed a yellow watercolor wash over the page and painted a watermelon on top. After that, it was a matter of getting the papers to lay on the page as I wanted them and taping them in place.

WEEKLY PLANNING

Weeklies may become the pages you create most often. Many people do their big-picture planning (yearly, quarterly, monthly) and their weeklies, and simply leave it at that, although some planner enthusiasts also make separate daily pages as well. Before you choose a weekly layout, think about the aspects of your life that you most want to plan. Do you need to be more on top of your household tasks? Make a box for that! Do you need a spot to organize your work meetings and goals? Create a section for work. Maybe you want to track your water intake or a new skill you are developing. Meal planning is another popular section. Once you have an idea of your key elements, browse different weekly layouts to find features to use in your own pages. The most common layout is a spread across two facing pages so there's plenty of space for everything you need to see. I find working on my weeklies on Saturday gives me time to figure out the layout and design. Then I go over it in marker on Sunday evening.

SIMPLE WEEKLIES

For many of us, though we are drawn to the pretty pages we see in other people's planners, we're just too busy to spend an hour or two designing our pages on a regular basis. But that doesn't mean they can't be beautiful and functional. Here I have pulled out some of my favorite simple or minimalistic pages to show you. I love the simplicity of using just black lines in my pages; it's clean, crisp, and uncluttered, and helps me focus on my goals.

TIP

Don't feel that you have to stick to just one layout! Play around with different designs over the course of a few weeks to see which one works the best for you.

Minimalism

I did this weekly in my narrow traveler's notebook insert, which means I had to get a bit creative with the space. I love how this forces me to be efficient—there's just no room for spaces between boxes or decorations but it still has everything I need to see in a week. I use the sections to write out lists and events that are coming up and I love combining my meal planning with my weekly spread. I added a small strip of black and white washi tape at the bottom and a few leaves in the dividers just because I was in the mood to be creative. This took me about 10 minutes to do and gave me everything I needed to see.

thursday

- ☐ Go get the mail
- ☐ Prepare Usborne books
- ☐ E-mails
- ☐ Bookwork
- ☐ Dinner: Chicken Parm

friday

- • Cassidy's birthday!
- ☐ Organize guest room
- ☐ Set up sheets
- ☐ Laundry
- ☐ Dinner: Spaghetti

Saturday

- ☐ Mom comes to town
- ☐ Get a birthday present
- ☐ Dinner: salad

Sunday

- ☐ Go to church
- • Family soccer game
- • Leftover day!

Notes: Figure out a gift for mom's birthday. Begin to work through boxes. Selah's xray is still waiting for results. No response from the hospital — follow up next week.

All Lined Up

I often use this technique to track my husband's work schedule because he works varying shifts. I love that this layout has so much space for checklists of things to do, upcoming events, or logs of "don't forgets!" I find it relaxing and a creative outlet to add a few sketches or doodles to my pages as I return to my book throughout the week, using images that speak to something that happened that day (see page 45 for an example of doodling my day).

Composition Style

Lest you think that planning should only be done in expensive notebooks, I wanted to show you a $1 composition notebook from a discount store. Although the pages are thin and the lines are large, you can easily use this for your weeklies. I did not even set this up ahead of time, but rather just made a new section for each day as I went through the week. This allowed me to get the most out of the page. You could easily do this as a spread on two pages if you want to add sections for habit trackers or meal planning or whatever else you need. Because I really am weather fixated, on the right-hand side I tracked the weather with the temperature and a little doodle showing what the weather was like that day.

COMPLEX WEEKLIES

While simple layouts are fast and relatively easy to create, more complex layouts offer you the ability to track and record much more information and to customize the space to work most effectively for you. Though they are more time-consuming to create, they are a great way to organize your thoughts and conceptualize the big picture of your week. Before you plan your layout, take a few minutes and make yourself a list of the regular things you want to track or record. Common sections I've included in my planner are water intake (I'm notorious for drinking more coffee than I do water), exercise log, sleep tracker, school schedules/due dates, work deadlines, time trackers, meal planning, step log (great for those of us with a fitness watch), weight loss graph, weather, mood, and many others. Once you know what you want to track, you can start designing your own layout or copy one of mine.

Split Spread

This weekly is one of my favorites. Although it offers a lot of detail, it only takes about 10 minutes to create. Many years ago I discovered that creating a short, prioritized list of things that had to be done before all else was key to a more productive and focused life. I have brought that same philosophy into my planning and often create a top three for my week. I also purchased a packet of large sticky notes from the dollar store and use one as my shopping list so I can take it out to the grocery store, come home, place a new sticky on the page, and create another list as the week progresses.

Time Tracker

Tracking how I spend my time helps me pinpoint time wasters and assess how I might be more efficient in the weeks to come. In this layout I decided to track my time with a simple graph underneath each day. I also wanted to make sure I had space for something I was thankful for each day. Keeping track of my husband's work schedule is one of the most important aspects of my week, though you could easily use a corner of your vertical planning boxes for weather or something else. I included my meal planning directly underneath the vertical daily boxes, which gave me more space for a shopping list.

MY STORY

This style of tracking my sleep is helpful because it offers a lot of information. Rather than simply tracking how many hours I got each night, I can see what time I woke up and went to bed, which allows me to assess what tweaks I can make to get the right amount of rest.

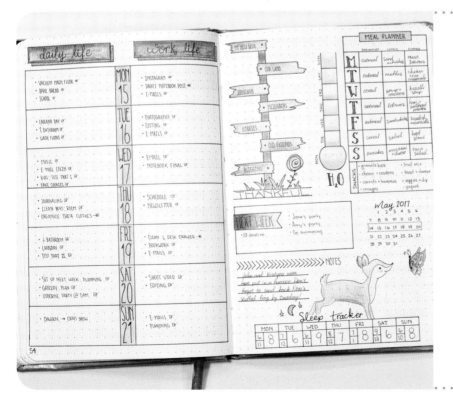

Pencil Crayon Flourish

Of all my detailed weeklies, this is my favorite. It offers me functionality as well as color and a few fun doodles. For this spread I didn't use any fancy watercolors or pens, I just raided my kids' pencil crayon stash. Keeping the dates in the middle permitted me to separate my personal and work lives, yet allowed me to see them both at once. My meal planner is the most detailed yet, including breakfast, lunch, dinner, and even snacks.

CREATIVE WEEKLIES

Creative planning has so many advantages. Not only is it a great way to express yourself without words, but it can also be a perfect stress reliever. The more time that you invest thinking about your upcoming week, planning it out, and even making it look pretty, the more clearly you will remember the goals and vision you laid out for yourself. Whether you are artistic or not, making something beautiful or bright or fun can make planning more interesting and customized to you. I'm a die-hard planner, but even I don't plan like this all the time! I find I go through stages where I become bored with my black-and-white pages and feel the urge to be more creative. But eventually I begin to miss the quick setup and simple beauty of my typical black-and-white pages. Let your layouts be what is right for you at the time.

Trees

I somehow keep on coming back to trees as a theme. I used the idea of the leaves touching as the wind blows through them as a symbol of the choices that I make creating a ripple effect through my days and weeks. I used the branches to plan out different parts of my day or even to write little notes to myself or memories I want to treasure.

MY STORY

Sometimes the hardest part of planning with a creative spread like this is filling it with a plan. It is so free and bright and artsy that trying to pair that with my more cerebral side seems to clash. I often hit a bit of a wall and can begin loving a background layout and then begin to dislike it as I "ruin it" with my plans. Instead of planning this week with bullet points and boxes, I decided to script my days using sentences detailing what I wanted to accomplish. I was still planning ahead, making goals and mentally processing how it would all fit, but doing it in a way that was more like a conversation with myself. It turned out to be a lot of fun!

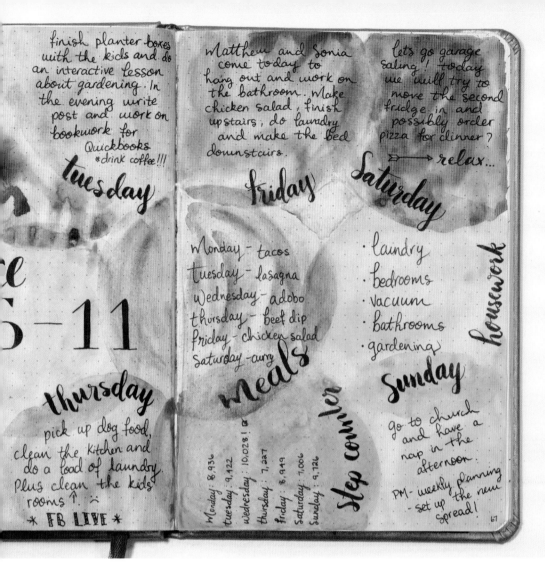

finish planter boxes with the kids and do an interactive lesson about gardening. In the evening write post and work on bookwork for Quickbooks *drink coffee!!!

tuesday

5 - 11

thursday

pick up dog food, clean the kitchen and do a load of laundry. Plus clean the kids rooms ↑ :)

* FB LIVE *

Matthew and Sonia come today to hang out and work on the bathroom. Make chicken salad, finish upstairs, do laundry and make the bed downstairs.

friday

Monday - tacos
tuesday - lasagna
Wednesday - adobo
thursday - beef dip
friday - chicken salad
Saturday - curry

meals

Monday: 8,936
tuesday: 9,122
Wednesday: 10,028
thursday: 7,327
friday: 8,949
Saturday: 7,006
Sunday: 9,726

Step counter

lets go garage saleing! today we will try to move the second fridge in and possibly order pizza for dinner?
→ relax...

Saturday

· laundry
· bedrooms
· vacuum
· bathrooms
· gardening

housework

Sunday

go to church and have a nap in the afternoon.
PM- weekly planning - set up the new spread!

67

Watercolor Background

I was inspired this week to try blending circles of different watercolors together. I overlapped the circles because it seems everything in my life connects with or overlaps something else. I sketched my circles out freehand with a pencil, which means that my circles aren't perfect. Again, this is symbolic of my life: imperfect, a work in progress. I dried each circle separately so the colors wouldn't run or blend beyond my control and painted lightly where they overlapped.

Scrapbooking

This is a style that I'm seeing more and more and while it's not typical for me, I wanted to at least try a free-style scrapbooking page. You don't have to be artsy to create an artistic spread AND most importantly, you don't have to love every spread you create. Not everything you try will resonate with you. Give yourself room to grow, my friend. It is going to make this planning thing a WHOLE lot more fun and less stressful!

MONTHLY LAYOUTS

No matter what planning system or strategy you are using, you are likely to incorporate monthly planning into your setup. Seeing the month at a glance is a key component to visualizing your goals and accomplishing what is important to you. It can be helpful to set up multiple months in advance so that you have somewhere to put appointments, though this is largely dependent on how you choose to organize your planner. There are a lot of different methods for planning your months, from grid view to a simple monthly log. Within each method are different styles and layouts you can use to make monthly plans that work for you.

TIP

If you have a grid or dot grid notebook, count the squares across and down on a page. If you are using a blank or lined journal, measure your page with a ruler instead. Write the result down somewhere as a cheat sheet. When you are making your calendar, use these numbers to divide the space evenly. I often sketch out the month in pencil to avoid making mistakes from miscounting. Give yourself room at the top for your headers, and at the bottom for notes if you desire.

Two-Page Layout

When considering your layout, first think about the main things you want to track each month. Maybe you want to keep it simple like this one, with big squares for your tasks and events and smaller boxes for notes, goals, to-dos, and a quick-reference small calendar. I prefer to be more artistic and detailed in my weeklies/dailies than my monthlies, so a spread like this is often what I choose. Before you begin setting up your grid, think about what day you want to start your week on, for example Sunday like a traditional calendar or Monday, the beginning of the workweek.

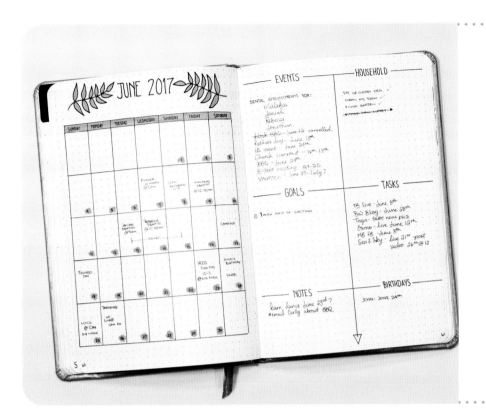

Single-Page Calendar

Although I always use two pages for a monthly, sometimes I arrange the calendar on one page and use the other side for more detailed planning. In this monthly, I organized my events, household tasks, goals, notes, and birthdays on the right-hand side. This page became a placeholder for tasks that I know I need to accomplish but doesn't tie me to a specific day those tasks need to be done. This allows for more flexible, open-ended planning.

Vertical Calendar

Instead of working my days across the page, here I placed them vertically down the page. It can take a little bit of getting used to, but I was surprised by how easily my brain began to work down, and I loved how I could see repeating events easily. On the left, I went super simple again, leaving space for only a few boxes.

Monthly Chronodex

We'll talk more about the Chronodex on page 70, but here you can see how easy it is to use this style for your monthly planning. Use a compass or trace something circular like a small bowl to create a circle, then divide it into 30 or 31 sections to represent each day of the month. It can be embellished with doodles, kept minimalistic, or even color coded. This only takes up about two-thirds of a page, which gives you room at the bottom and on the facing page to fit in other planning elements, events, and tasks.

Minimalistic Monthly Log

The simplest way to set up a monthly log is with a typical two-page design. For events, write the numbers 1 to 31 (or whatever day the month ends on) and the first letter of the day of the week beside it, highlighting the first day of the week with a different color or a simple line. Set aside the second page for monthly tasks. Refer back to the events and tasks in your weekly or daily planning throughout the month. I expanded on the original bullet journal idea shown on page 35, and organized my weeks on the left for notes and tasks, leaving the right side open for appointments and events.

NOVEMBER

WORK | HOME | LIFE

1
2
3
4
5
6
7
8
9
10
11
12
13
14
15
16
17
18
19
20
21

TRACKERS

| W | V | R | Wr | I's | A | 6 | P |

GOALS

I ADORE *spontaneity* SO LONG AS IT IS CAREFULLY *planned!*

NOTES

Detailed Monthly

If you have a lot of elements you want to include in your monthly planning, consider a more detailed layout. I created columns for three different aspects of my life: work, home, and personal. On the other side of the page I created my monthly tracker where I refer back to daily tasks to complete. The spaces on my daily tracker section line up with the days on the left page, so I didn't need to re-draw all my numbers and days. A simple color-coded key helps me track the different items such as water, vitamins, reading, and writing. In the right-hand margin I still had space for my monthly goals, a doodle, and a quote that inspires me.

Modified Monthly

Instead of separating my daily tasks and events into three sections, I used a very simple layout with a frame that lines up with the first page. I still had room for birthdays, tasks, and goals in the right hand margin. This is one of my favorite monthly layouts—I love the graphic look of this page.

Single Pager

While I am pretty set on two-page monthly layouts in my own planner, a one-page layout is possible. This layout displays a small month-at-a-glance to refer to in weekly planning and has a small section for different tasks and events. Spreads like this can work well if you do your monthly planning on a month-by-month basis, rather than quarterly or biannually. You could use the previous page to do a monthly cover design if you have the space and feel artsy. I had already done a watercolor wash on this page and I decided to utilize it by adding a quote.

In Black and White

Here is an example of a more artistic layout you could try using just your black pen. I decided to do a very simple vertical grid calendar on the right-hand side (meaning my week works down instead of across). On the left I created a fun cover for the month as well as my calendar at a glance, important dates, and goals. You don't need color or paint to do a beautiful page.

Artistic Notebook

If you are feeling like being creative in your planning, try a monthly art page. I came up with this spread after playing a game on my kids' iPad. I created colored bubbles on the left-hand side as my calendar, and on the right I placed a simple habit tracker, to-do notebook, goals section, as well as notes. I used a few different sizes of my Copic pens, my Tombow brush pens for the coloring, and a stencil for the circles. This was easy and fun without being too time-consuming.

QUARTERLY PLANNING

Big picture planning is a snapshot of what is coming up. It is your quick, at-a-glance tool that you will use when you set up your monthly spreads. It can be set up however you wish, but I generally approach this in either four-month or six-month increments—neither of which is actually a quarter. That's just another example of how flexible planning is! The main purpose behind big-picture planning is to slot in events, appointments, due dates, and notes months in advance. While some people organize their planners with specific spaces for each month, other people plan day by day. With quarterly or bi-yearly planning, it's not necessary to set everything up ahead of time. You'll be able to view multiple months at once to see where things overlap or connect.

FUTURE LOG

The future log is a bullet journal method developed by Ryder Carroll, and is fast and simple. In essence, it is a simple list with four to six months on a two-page spread. Over time, people have adapted this system with mini calendars, sections, dates, color coding, and vertical logs. You can start this process whenever you start your journal. For example, if you started your planner in August, you would begin your future log

Vertical Future Log
I love having a mini calendar with my future log. Being able to quickly reference dates when I'm at an appointment is critical for me. I can set up an entire month using nothing but my future log, which means I can do it anywhere! In a vertical future log you have room for notes at the bottom or you can extend your columns to give you more space for planning. Your future log will likely be used mainly for appointments and events, so take that into account when deciding how much space you need.

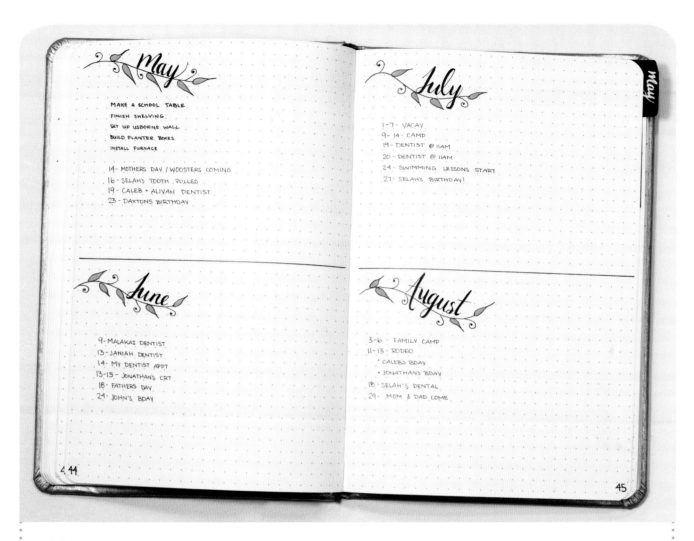

Minimalistic Future Log

For this layout all you need to do is write out your months and draw a line to separate each month. It can take about five minutes to set up (depending on how much time you take with your lettering) and you're done! You can either list events and tasks with bullets; use a key to organize events, tasks, and notes; or even use checkboxes. Draw a line through each item as you complete it or an arrow to show you need to migrate it to another month if you didn't get it done.

with September because you will already be doing a monthly for August. These logs are usually done in the front of your planner, ahead of your monthlies, weeklies, and dailies, and are repeated throughout your planner as often as needed. Before you begin, decide how much space you want for this layout, how much time you have (keep in mind you will only be doing this every four to six months), and how detailed you want it to be.

CALENDEX

The Calendex is basically a calendar combined with an index. It was developed by Eddy Hope as an adapted future log. It is less about planning specific events and more about logging when they happen. The original system uses all twelve months on a two-page spread, but you can do as many months at once as you like. When you have an event,

Original Calendex
Once you know how many months you want, create columns, then write the numbers 1 through 31 on the left side of your columns (just once per page). Place lines in each of the columns to separate the weeks within the month. You'll notice there are some shaded-out boxes on the bottom; that is simply because not every month has 31 days. Hope has shared that he crosses out days on his Calendex as he goes so that he can quickly see where he is when looking back.

go to your next blank page in your planner and write the event down and any notes or details about that event. Then go back to your Calendex and write in the page number on a box. This way you can see more at a glance and find exactly where it is as you go.

ALASTAIR METHOD

Developed by Alastair Johnston, this popular method is a simple and effective way to plan future events. It uses a series of columns to create "containers" for information that are easy to update. This is usually done in six-month increments, but like everything else in planning, you can adapt this to your needs.

Calendex/Future Log Hybrid
Because of the way I organize my planner, I don't like to write events on a blank page or place them in my planner until I have my monthlies or weeklies set up. So I write in the event and add the page number once I put it into my planner. This has two benefits: It allows me to plan for the future without disturbing my planner layout, and it creates an index so I can easily refer to the event.

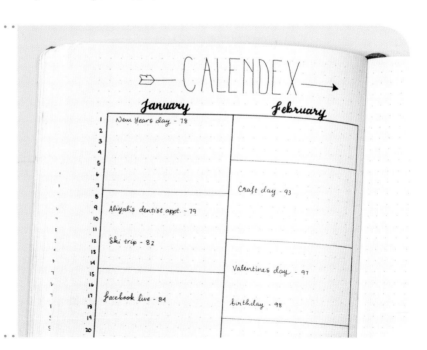

My Alastair

Create a series of columns on the left-hand side of your page with the months you want to see in advance. Next to these columns, write out events and tasks as they come up and put a dot next to the month in which they should happen. When you are ready for your monthly planning, find the dots that are associated with your current month and add them in. You can even color code the dots so that it is easier to spot them quickly. Being able to add things as I think of them is a huge bonus for me.

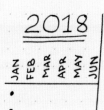

JANUARY - JUNE ALASTAIR METHOD LOG

JAN 9 - ALIYAH'S DENTAL
JAN 12 @ 9AM SKI TRIP
FEB. 17 @ 6PM DINNER
SCHOOL FUN DAY JUN 24 @ 11AM
APR. 6 - TRIP OUT OF TOWN

Alastair/Calendex Hybrid

While the Alastair method gives you freedom and flexibility, some people prefer something that is more visually organized. As a variation, you can place items into the log on the right-hand side of the page, while putting the left-hand side of the page into the Calendex. Now when it comes to setting up your months, you simply have to look on your Calendex and index which page you are planning the events on. Essentially you get future planning, monthly planning, and indexing all in a single two-page spread, for months at a time!

YEARLY PLANNING

Yearly planning pages are usually created at the front of your planner. The most common method is to simply create a mini calendar spread. Some people like to do something similar to the future log, with space to write out their plans for the year, but the method you choose depends on whether you want to have room for a small future log, or want to see just your calendars. Having your monthly calendars for the year all drawn out in advance will save you time each month. It can also serve as an easy reference when you want to find something quickly.

Yearly Mini Calendars
There are so many options for this. You can color code your calendars, making them ornate or simple. You can draw little boxes around your calendars, or create them in columns. You will be referring to this spread a LOT, so figure out something that appeals to you and take your time with it.

Detailed Yearly
I found creating separate boxes to be a useful approach in yearly planning. I recommend penciling it in first, which may sound mundane but you would be surprised how easy it is to make mistakes when you are repeating yourself over and over. Once it is penciled in, you can go over it in pen at your leisure.

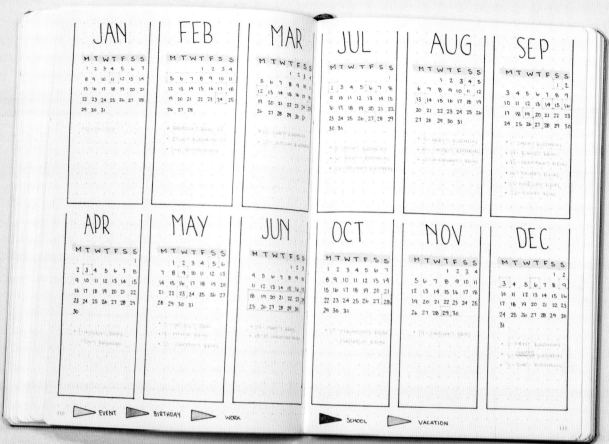

Yearly Vertical Future Log

This combines the value of a year at a glance with the space to write important events that are coming up throughout the year. You won't have enough space for detailed planning, but it does afford you the ability to jot down key events and, in a pinch, this can even be used to replace a future log if you don't like the idea of repeating yourself.

Yearly with Events

This layout combines the simplicity of seeing the entire year in those adorable little mini calendars with a condensed future log on the right. You could use these boxes on the right to write down events or even use them like a calendex. To do this, write the date and the page number where you will find more information about that month. You could even use it to create big-picture goals for each month that you want to accomplish or write a quote of the month. However you use it, it is easy to refer to what you need when doing your daily planning pages. I hand drew all of this in with no ruler and I love the little shakes and movement of the lines.

SPECIALTY PLANNING

Some people use their planners solely to organize their schedules, but many more people find their planners useful in organizing and streamlining many other aspects of their lives. Whatever is important to you can be a part of your planner. For example, I not only use my planner as a calendar, but I also use it for laying out plans for my work life, for organizing family events, and even for self-improvement.

HABIT TRACKERS

A common element you will have seen on many of my planner pages is a habit tracker. It's a powerful tool that helps me work toward a goal, establish a new habit, or break a bad habit. Many people create separate pages for their habit trackers, others incorporate this section into their monthlies. Others use habit trackers by placing them in smaller chunks in their weekly or daily pages. Before you decide which strategy you want to use, consider your planning rhythm. For example, while I like the idea of setting up my habit trackers in my monthly spreads, I find that I lack the discipline to come back and fill in a tracker each day. I work better with my habit trackers included directly within the pages I am currently working on, and then I transfer those over to a monthly habit tracker to see at a glance how I am faring with my plan to form or break a habit. As with everything in the planner world, habit trackers vary from a simple page with a header to elaborate and detailed designs.

Mood Tracker

These are very popular as a tool to become more mindful of emotions and attitudes, so we can learn how they effect our day. I like to cross-reference them with my daily planning or journal pages. When I do this, I see clear patterns between mood and productivity. You may also see other connections in your health, your sleep, and even your diet depending on how much information you put in your planner. I've discovered that the days that I struggled the most with frustration or sadness are my least productive.

Single Page Habit Tracker
One option is to decide all the different habits you want to begin or improve on. I recommend starting with daily habits to help you isolate your most pressing priorities. In this habit tracker, I used a black pen and some pencil crayon to create boxes that are 10 squares across and 4 squares down. That left me with enough space for 30 days (not quite 31, but I kept it simple). I wrote out the habit I wanted to work on and marked the days I succeeded in that habit with a pencil crayon.

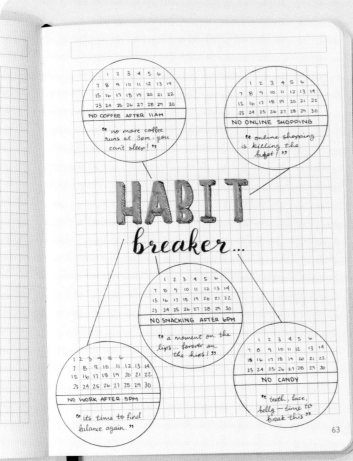

Habit Breaker
The habit breaker is similar to a habit tracker but instead of keeping track of a habit I want to make, I keep track of the days I manage to NOT do something I want to quit. Again, I made 30 days to color in with a pencil crayon or marker but this time with circles instead of rectangles. I made this more of a mind map style, with everything connecting to the habit breaker header in the middle. I began by writing the things I wanted to stop (coffee after 11 a.m., online shopping, snacking after 6 p.m., eating candy, and working after 5 p.m.) and I also wrote an inspirational quote, funny remark, or word of encouragement to myself at the top. This made actionable steps for me ... one day at a time!

TIME TRACKERS

Telling ourselves what we want to do is really just step one in setting ourselves up for success. Remember the quote, "A goal without a plan is just a wish"? We can make countless lists of what we want to accomplish, but if we haven't made actionable steps for ourselves and set realistic goals, we aren't going to be successful. Time trackers give us a method for tracking where our moments are spent, so we can identify time wasters, weed them out, and become more efficient. Alternatively, time trackers can be used to organize sections of our day so that we can refer to our planner and know at a glance what we should be working on during that block. These two approaches give us tools to put these lofty plans of ours into practice. They can motivate us, propel us into being better stewards of our time, and help us become more realistic about what we can accomplish in a defined period. Setting up a tracker in your planner every once in a while can be a healthy check and balance in the natural flow of your life. Even if you are more of a free-flowing planner than a detailed one, I still encourage you to try tracking the time you spend on various tasks in a typical day. Then you can easily see how you can tweak your routine or schedule to fit in whatever is most important to you. In these next pages, I'll share five different techniques you can bring into your planner to track your time.

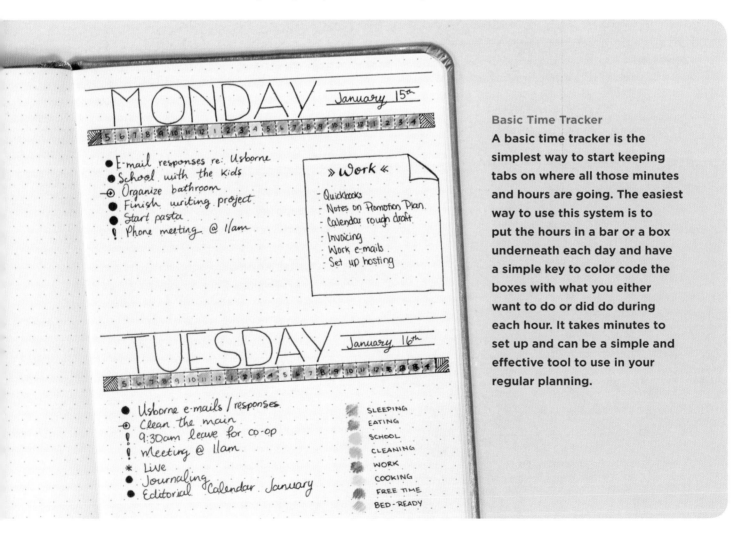

Basic Time Tracker
A basic time tracker is the simplest way to start keeping tabs on where all those minutes and hours are going. The easiest way to use this system is to put the hours in a bar or a box underneath each day and have a simple key to color code the boxes with what you either want to do or did do during each hour. It takes minutes to set up and can be a simple and effective tool to use in your regular planning.

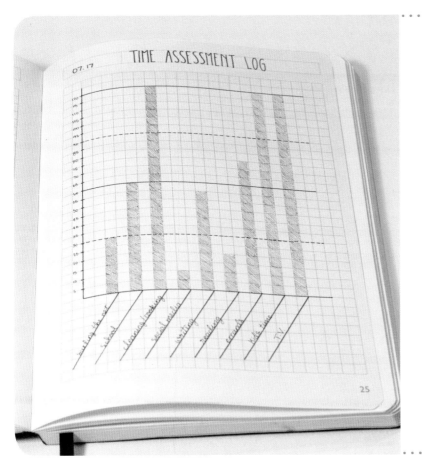

Time Graph

A time graph is a detailed layout of how you spent your time. It's a great periodic assessment tool. Every month or two, create a time graph in your planner for one day. Keep track of what you did during the day, even if it's by creating simple voice notes on your phone that you note down at the end of the day. This helps you identify key time wasters that are holding you up, and times of day that you are more motivated vs. your natural slumps (i.e., caffeine dip or the afternoon doldrums). You can use this information to create a more realistic "ideal day" in your planner that takes your own natural rhythm, mood, and routine into account and prioritizes your main goals.

Time Ladder

The time ladder can be made on the left, middle, or right side of the page. It is a glorified schedule that can be used in multiple ways. You can use it to track how you spent your time. You could also use the time ladder as your daily planner. For this purpose, my preference is to create it in the middle of the page so one side is used for planning and the other side is used for noting what actually happened. Alternatively, you can also use it to create your ideal day. As I do my regular planning, I find it very useful to go back to my ideal day and use it to create more realistic goals for myself or to assess how my priorities and goals change over the year.

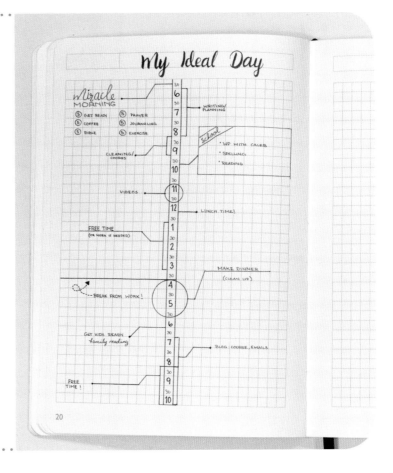

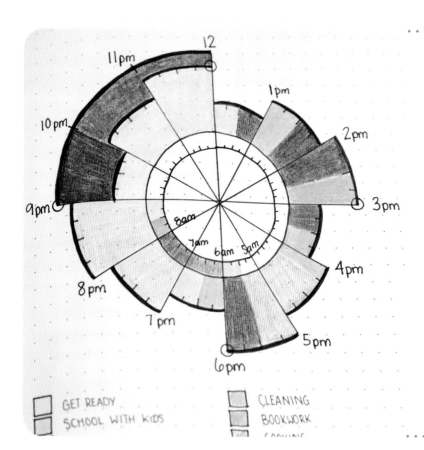

GET READY
SCHOOL WITH KIDS

CLEANING
BOOKWORK

Chronodex

The Chronodex method was first introduced by Patrick Ng. Think of it as a clockface separated into 12 pie slices that each represent an hour. Many people who use the Chronodex regularly purchase a stamp or use stickers so that they don't have to draw the slices. Some people create a key and color code the slices. Others just write directly into the slices. What makes this so effective is that you can tell the time of day and what you should be doing with a glance. For me, the downside is that you are limited to 12 hours! This system focuses your planning on the main part of your day and forces you to stop after 12 hours, automatically scheduling downtime into your routine.

Spiraldex

The Spiraldex was developed by Kent from Oz. It is a color-coded index that has a bit more flexibility than the Chronodex because you can create as many sections and make it as big as you want. Some people make two sets of lines in their circles, allowing them to plan for two things happening at once (reading a report while getting a haircut, for example). I set mine up to start at 5 a.m. and end at 12 a.m. There are typically three dots along the edge that represent 15-minute increments, so that you can block your time. Without a stamp or printable sheet, it can be awkward to set up, but it is a handy way of setting your priorities and yet still leaving flexibility and room for spontaneity in your day.

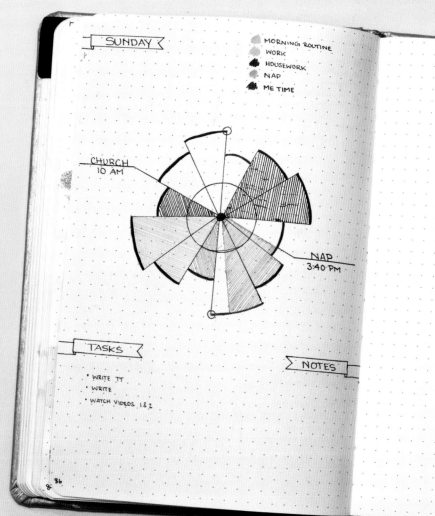

MEAL PLANNING

Meal planning is one of my regular activities in my planning routine. I often incorporate it into a small section or area of my weekly planning so that I know what's for dinner every night that week, and I use that to create my shopping list. Whether you are cooking for one or for ten, taking the time to think about your meals saves time, aggravation, and lots of money (less takeout!). Knowing what we are doing for dinner helps my whole day run more smoothly because I plan my routine around it, either starting dinner in the slow cooker in the morning or knowing what time it needs to go on the stove or in the oven in the evening. When I sit down to do my nightly updates in my planner, I take a quick look to see if I need to pull anything from the freezer for the next day.

Because there is such a wide variety of ways to do meal planning, from just sketching out your dinner ideas to planning all your meals and snacks, I've included a wide variety of ideas you could try in your own planner. Some of these are easy to incorporate into your weekly planning, while others are collections that can be re-used over and over. Before choosing a style to use in your planner, think about whether you need to plan all meals or just dinners, and whether you want your shopping list in your planner or a scratch pad you can copy off your planner and take to the store. This will help you figure out how much space you need, as well as whether bringing it into your weeklies and dailies, or creating a separate page is best for you.

Meal Planning Card

If you only need to plan your dinners, try something simple and incorporate it into your weekly or daily planning. Here I used black cardstock and a white gel pen to get a chalkboard look in my planner to shout out "menu!" In this layout, I did a light watercolor wash where I organized my weekly goals (labeling the day I wanted to accomplish them), taped in my meal plan with some fun washi tape, and began setting up some daily sections on the other side of the page. Keeping the menu small like this means that you can see it right in the middle of your weekly planning without searching for a specific collection you made.

Meal Plan Notebook
In this spacious layout, I created a weekly meal plan on one page, leaving the other side free for either weekly or daily plans. There is enough room for breakfasts, lunches, and dinners. I had fun with some doodles beside each box and a little banner in the corner to label what they represent. You could do this in any size notebook, but pay attention to how many squares or lines you have to ensure you have room for all your days and spaces between boxes.

Grocery List
This layout is based on one of the most popular inserts I've made. On the left-hand side I have a place for each of my days separated by an arrow. The apples give me space to plan out snacks. The bonus of this spread is that there is a huge box left for my grocery list. This means that I can set up my plan, make my list, and bring it with me to the store. I won't forget about a meal or snack because it is all laid out for me. I LOVE this spread!

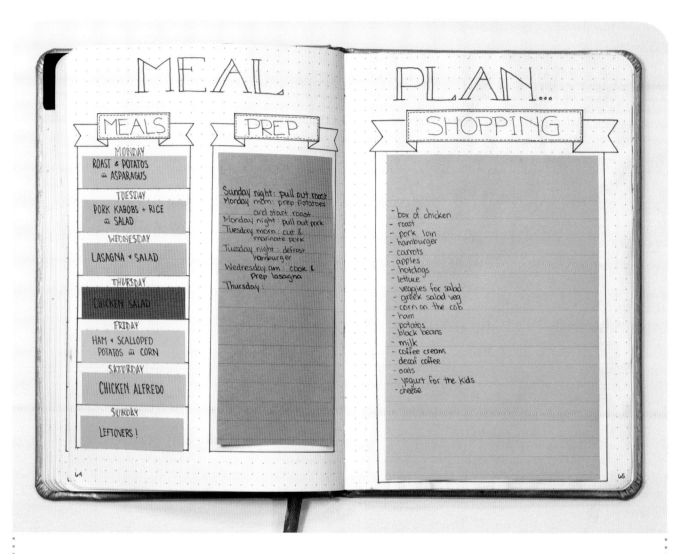

MEAL PLAN...

MEALS

MONDAY
ROAST & POTATOS ∞ ASPARAGUS

TUESDAY
PORK KABOBS + RICE ∞ SALAD

WEDNESDAY
LASAGNA + SALAD

THURSDAY
CHICKEN SALAD

FRIDAY
HAM + SCALLOPED POTATOS ∞ CORN

SATURDAY
CHICKEN ALFREDO

SUNDAY
LEFTOVERS!

PREP

Sunday night: pull out roast
Monday morn: prep potatoes and start roast
Monday night: pull out pork
Tuesday morn: cut & marinate pork
Tuesday night: defrost hamburger
Wednesday am: cook & prep lasagna
Thursday:

SHOPPING

- box of chicken
- roast
- pork loin
- hamburger
- carrots
- apples
- hotdogs
- lettuce
- veggies for salad
- greek salad veg
- corn on the cob
- ham
- potatos
- black beans
- milk
- coffee cream
- decaf coffee
- oats
- yogurt for the kids
- cheese

Sticky Note

There's a reason this type of spread is so popular: It's ingenious! Build the framework with various rectangles the size of both small and larger sticky notes. This spread is 100 percent reusable, so it's really more of a collection, but I thought it would be helpful to include it here. You can return to this place week after week to plan out your meals. You can organize your meals, your prep (what you should do the night before or morning of), as well as your shopping list. When you're ready to head to the grocery store, simply pull off your shopping list and go!

MY STORY

In my next planner I intend to expand on this concept and have ideas for side dishes, quick baking projects, breakfast, lunch, and dinner, all broken down by ingredient. These ideas can also be incorporated with the types of meal planning collections shown on pages 7 and 87. There are a ton of options with these spreads, and the more detail you can include, the easier meal planning will be!

WORK PLANNING

These days, so many of us are working—at least part time—at a home office, making our personal and professional lives ever more intertwined. A custom planner can help you separate your work and personal life, or integrate them more fully. Some people find that separating the two helps them be more engaged in each area. Others find it frustrating not to see all their obligations and tasks at once.

Whichever way is right for you, a work planner can help you keep track of meetings and deadlines, income and expenses, mileage and vehicle upkeep, growth and goals, clients and coworkers, and more. Because it's custom made, you can set it up to be specific to you and targeted to your specific industry and lifestyle.

Take a few minutes to brainstorm what will make it most effective for you. Define your industry, job, and role. Think about the items you should track and organize. Do you need somewhere to list tasks and due dates, or a place to scribble ideas and meeting minutes? How much space do you need? You will likely want to have some work-specific collections on top of your regular weekly and daily planning. As a blogger, my collections include tracking my affiliate income, relevant keywords and hashtags, stats, goals, brainstorming, sponsors, reviews, blog post ideas, income and expense tracker (to be entered in my accounting software), as well as a brainstorming sheet for each blog post I write (keywords, content, headers, the URL, etc.). Once you have an idea what kind of sections you want, you can begin creating layouts for them.

MY STORY

I find that the more perfect we try to make our planners, the less we use them when we really need them. For example, when I need to jot down something during a phone call, I have to stop myself from reaching for scrap paper. The perfectionist in me still resists scrawling in my pretty planner. Of course, I usually lose that little piece of paper—and the critical information I wrote on it. If it's important enough to jot down, write it in your planner! Function over beauty is the goal.

Growth and Stats Tracker
This layout, though old, should give you an idea of how you could use your planner to track your growth and business goals. I love putting these two spreads together because I can see how my goals are impacting my actual growth.

Mileage Tracker

Another idea is a mileage tracker, to help you keep track for tax time. These can be super simple, though I recommend bringing your planner with you if you are doing this so that you can fill it in on the go.

Business Routine

I find it helpful to have a business routine rather than a schedule. Because I work at home, every day is a bit different depending on what is going on in my personal life, so having a master plan of tasks that I gradually move through where I can fit them helps me stay focused and on task. I also created some actionable steps with daily tasks, monthly tasks, a planning strategy, etc. I refer to this often when I am just spinning my wheels, struggling with where to start.

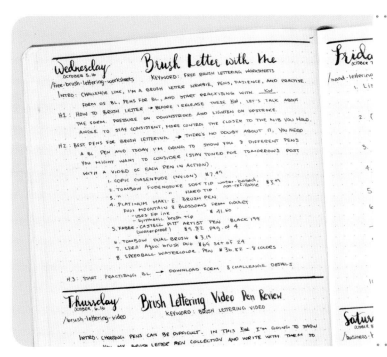

Ongoing Work Tasks

This shows how I plan out my blog posts, which is an important part of my business. It's actually a bit of a mess. I focus more on content and organizing my thoughts than what it looks like. I find that taking the time to do a rough outline of my post, find my keyword, log the date it will go live, etc. helps save a TON of time while I am writing. It allows me to follow a plan rather than trying to decide how it will look on the go. This type of layout can be used to take meeting notes, or to outline presentations or reports.

STUDENT PLANNING

In my planning and journaling journey I have encountered a HUGE group of planners who took up this practice because they needed to keep track of their classes, exams, assignments, notes, and study groups, and to keep an eye on their grades and study habits. Students have an enormous amount of information they must keep at hand. Here are some simple layouts that can be a big help.

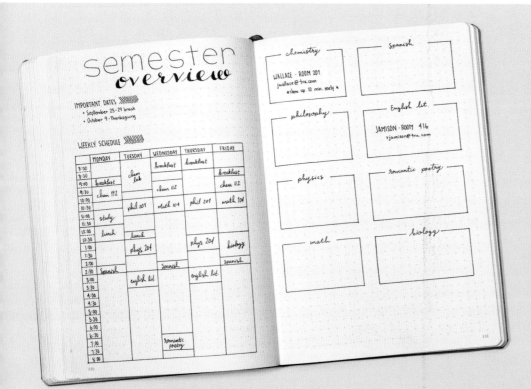

Semester Overview

As your semester fills up, an overview can act like a future log, helping you see the entire semester at a glance. In this layout, I included a key to conserve space as well as small calendars and space beside each one. While this isn't enough space to write down every assignment, it is great for keeping track of cancelled classes, large projects that are due, exams, breaks, and more. On the other side of the spread I included a class schedule as well.

Assignment Tracker

Assignments and quizzes can be overwhelming, especially if you have a heavy course load. An assignment tracker can help you figure out due dates that are coming up for each class and you can even color code it to keep track of your average grades (though I'll show you a grade tracking system you can use instead if you prefer something that is more detailed). This is a very easy way to see all your projects at a glance. You can use this when you are setting up your weekly and daily planning pages.

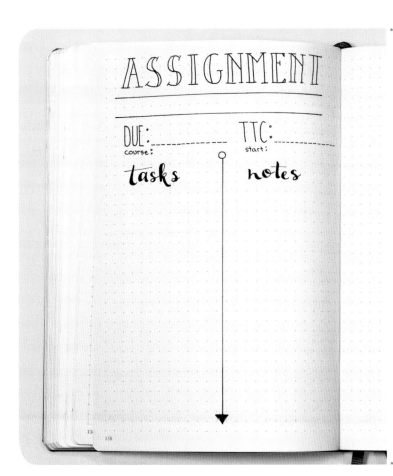

Assignment Planner

For large-scale assignments, it might be helpful to set aside a page or two to plan out exactly what you need to do. An assignment planner can include the due date, the course name, how long you think it will take, when you plan on starting, various tasks you need to complete for the assignment, and any notes you compile along the way. If you create a page like this in advance, be sure to assign a firm start date to your paper or project that will give you plenty of time to complete it before the due date.

Grade Tracker

If you want to use a grid to keep track of grades, something like this is simple to set up and use. You can create one for each class or keep it simple and just have a list of grades achieved in each class. How you set this up will depend on what you are looking to track (i.e., overall average or individual grades per class). Tallying up your average in the last column can help you stay on track with your goals and see throughout the semester where you are and how you could improve.

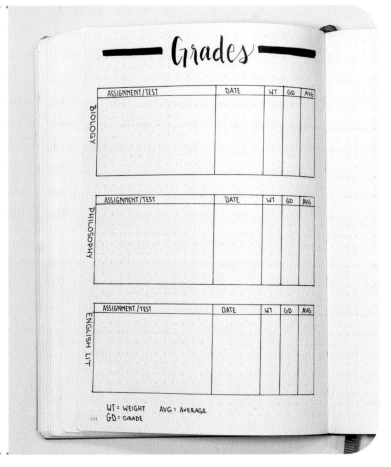

FAMILY
fun night ideas...

- Sherlock Night
- Culture Night

- Swimming
- Ice-Skating
- Water Park
- Bike Ride
- Movie Night
- Campfire
- Story Night
- RAK
- Extreme Couponing
- Walk
- Games
- Craft
- Journaling
- Free Write
- Scavenger Hunt
- Hide and Seek
- Lego Night
- Capture the Flag
- Soccer
- Basketball
- Trampoline
- Star Gazing
- Nerf Gun Night
- Puppet Show N
- Theatre Night
- Monologue
- Show and-Te
- Make a Fam
- Charades
- Karaoke
- Dance Par
- Book Clu

24.

≪ CHEAP DATE IDEAS ≫

- Picnic
- Go for a walk
- Trailer Date
- Library
- Thrift Store
- Movie Night
- Board Game
- Workout
- Star Gazing
- Book Club
- Museum / Art
- Dancing

Re-assess my business goals and priorities. What should my focus be? Make a list of what is making money, what I feel I'm being asked to focus on and how to go about it. Create new goals and go for them! ~Business Thoughts

BRAIN dump

54   ← 16

COLLECTIONS

• • •

One of my favorite parts of planning is making collections. To me, it is a place to organize my thoughts and keep track of the details of my life. When I set up a collection, especially one that is a list of things to accomplish, I give that subject all my attention and think about how I can make the tasks related to it easier or more streamlined. Not only are my collections the most useful and reliable parts of my planner, but they are also one of my key strategies for day-to-day success. Here I'll share lots of different examples from simple lists to artistic and detailed catalogs. I encourage you to flip through and look at the photos first, then read the background on the ones that you are drawn to for information on how and why I created them. This may well spark a new idea for you. Use the list from page 25 to brainstorm some of the collections you want to include in your planner and take a look at how diverse those can be!

PLANNING

For me, planning collections are instrumental in the day-to-day success of planning. I love adding creative flair with doodles and designs, and these collections give me inspiration and ideas when I am not sure where to start. They also help me keep track of important information that I need, such as a general planning routine so I don't miss something, my favorite supplies and where to get them, quotes I want to use in my daily and weekly spreads, and more.

Doodle Ideas

I love adding little doodles to my regular planning pages. Although I generally keep my doodles simple, I find that I enjoy using graphics and regularly need new ideas. To save searching through thousands of pins online, I created a simple doodle idea collection when I was feeling inspired in the front of my journal. I organized them by topic/subject so I can quickly find something that fits what I want to represent in my planner. If you like to use these kinds of touches on your pages, creating a reference will make choosing decorative elements for your pages much easier. If you need help, check out the traceable doodles starting on page 137.

Banners and Headers

Two of the elements I use the most in my planner are banners and headers. On many of my pages I use a variety of headers and accents to make my titles a bit more interesting. When I get bored with the same old designs, I pop over to this page and select a new design. You'd be surprised how easy it is to forget the different sketches you've tried.

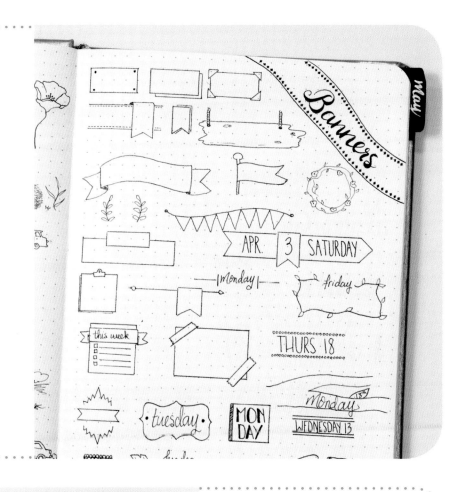

Hand-Lettering Combos

When you are creating and designing your own planner, having a collection for a variety of hand-lettering combinations can serve as both inspiration and a framework. I generally have a few different fonts that I am drawn to, but I tend to get bored with the same look over and over. Seeing some different combinations gives me a fresh look in my pages, without wasting time searching on the internet for ideas.

Planning Routines

Having a routine is the only way planning makes sense for me. While I LOVE the creativity, expression, and originality of a handmade planner, I struggled with consistency at first. I found that creating a planning routine that broke down my tasks into small, easily managed chunks helped me make planning an everyday habit.

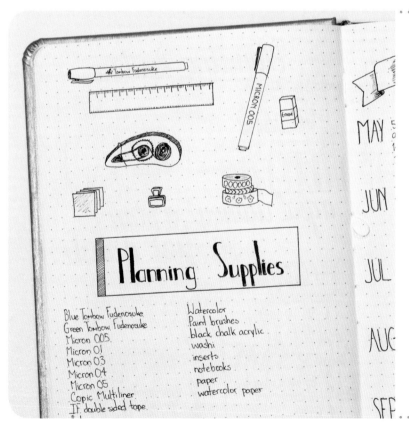

Planning Supplies

I like to make a list of some of my more common supplies and refer to that every once in a while when I am running low on one thing or another. I hate to get home from the store to find I needed something else that I didn't purchase. In the beginning, when you are still new to planning, creating a collection like this can help you remember the names and brands of supplies people tell you about, or great finds you've stumbled across.

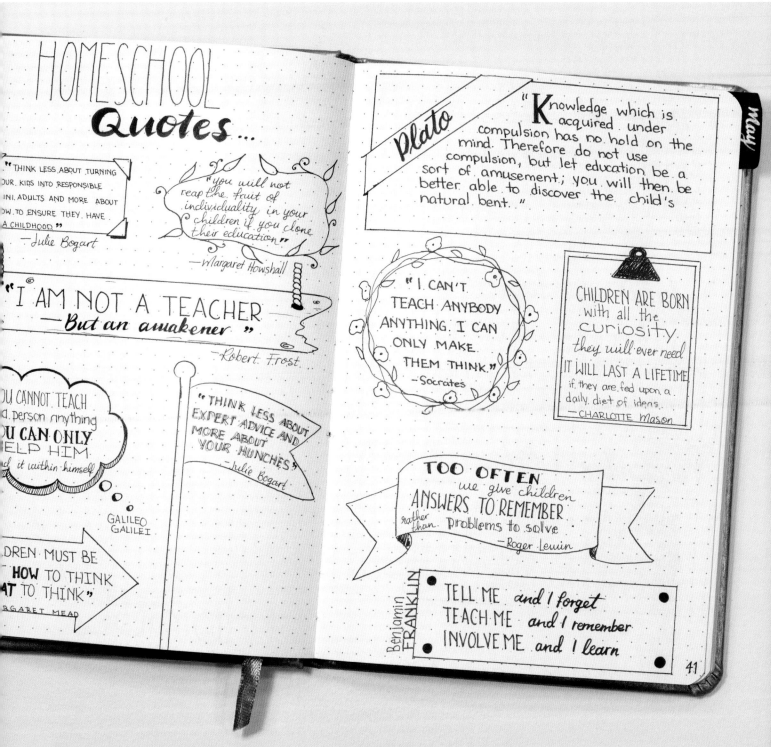

Quotes

I decided to do a homeschool quote collection because it makes sense for my life, but I wanted to show it in this section because it can easily be tweaked for your needs. Maybe a collection of inspirational quotes, or parenting quotes, or work quotes, or humorous quotes are just what you need for your weeklies or dailies. This is a great place to use those banners and doodles you organized in your banner collection!

FAMILY LIFE

My family life is a bit chaotic, to say the least. I am so busy with kids and teaching said kids, and trying to keep up with the home and meals and just life in general that I tend to think of these collections as my analog brain! They allow me to have everything in one place and to keep track of those details that make me look like supermom. I firmly believe that behind every supermom is a well-used planner!

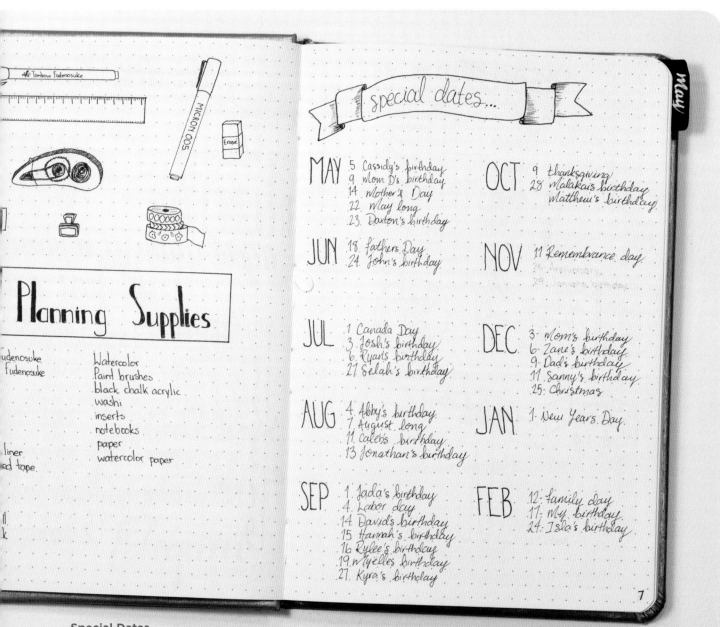

Special Dates

I use this page all the time. Every. Single. Month. I have such a large, extended family that I needed to organize birthdays, anniversaries, and long weekends into one page so I can see at a glance what is coming up, who needs a phone call or a gift, or when I should be planning an event. This simple list has become one of my most crucial collections.

My Size

I have found that different brands fit differently, so to simplify online shopping, I put together a simple collection to keep track of my measurements, partly for my sake and partly for my husband's. He often peeks at my planner to find out what is happening that week and uses this page to refer to when he wants to buy me something. (It may be rare, but a girl's got to be prepared!)

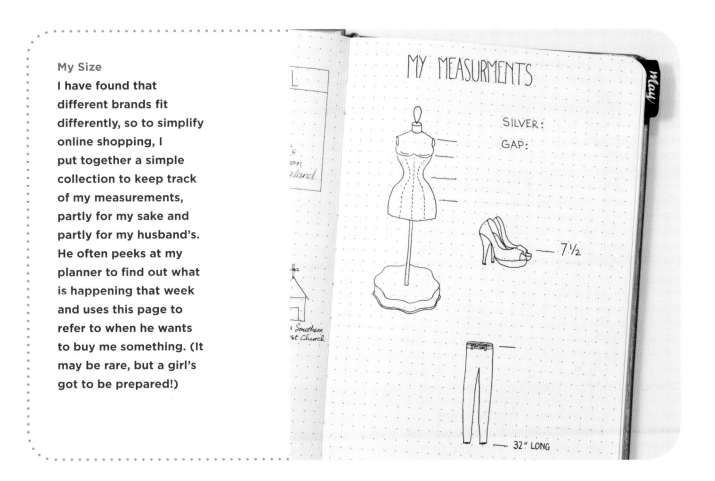

Family Measurements

I also went ahead and created two more pages of family sizes that I wrote in with pencil. This way as my kids' sizes change I can adjust them. It is a lifesaver when it comes to online shopping or when I spot an unexpected deal. No more wondering if that bargain will fit!

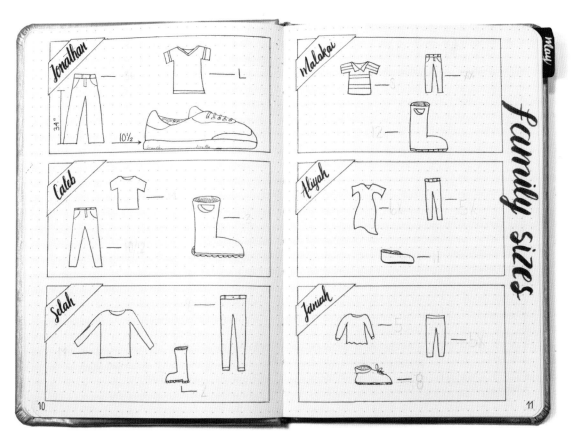

Memories Collection

Each month I try to do a memory spread, or things I loved about that month, or a recap collection—something that helps me visualize key moments in the years that are flying by. We like doing these together as a family as we reflect on our favorite things, our not-so-favorite things, and things we simply don't want to forget.

Things Kids Say

I love keeping track of the crazy, cute, and downright inappropriate things that my kids say. If I don't write them down, I know I won't remember them down the road. I love the simplicity and fun doodle element of this collection.

things I love about...

she is affectionate
Her Smile!
she is goofy
she is Gentle!
Her compassion!
laugh
she is sensitive!
Her determination!

Things I Love About...

As I was thinking about different things I wanted to focus on this year, I decided to do a different take on a gratitude collection. Instead of a broad-spectrum list of things I am thankful for, I created a page for each member of my family and things I love about them. There is no day that isn't improved by reviewing this list.

MENU

BRAINSTORM

INSTANT POT	20:00	30:00	40:00	50:00	60:00	CROCK	ROAST
POT ROAST	SALMON + RICE	SATAY STIR-FRY	SPAGHETTI	MAC + CHEESE	SHEPHERDS PIE	CHILI	ROAST
MAC + CHEESE	CHICKEN SPAGHETTI	WARM POTATO SALAD	CHICKEN KATSU	POTATO-LEEK SOUP	LASAGNA	TACOS	ROASTED POTATOS
CARNITAS	PASTA SALAD	NACHOS	CAJUN CHICKEN	CURRY CHICKEN	FRIED CHICKEN	PORK IN A BUN	TURKEY
CHILI	CHICKEN ALFREDO	CHICKEN PARM	SANTA FE SALAD	VEGGIE STEW	HOMEMADE PIZZA	HAMBURGER SOUP	CHICKEN
BEEF STEW	QUINOA BOWL	SZECHUAN CHICKEN	BROCOLLI SOUP	SPRING ROLLS	STEAK	TURKEY STEW	RIBS + BAKED POT
APPLE SAUCE	CHICKEN ASPARAGUS	CHICKEN MARSALA	HALIBUT + FRIES		CHICKEN ADOBO	LENTIL SOUP	PORK LOIN
CHANA MASALA	STIR-FRY	GARLIC LIME CH.			BREAKFAST		
BARBACOA	FRIED RICE	SWEDISH MEATBALLS			GREEK POTATOS		
LENTIL SOUP	LO MEIN	FAJITAS					
BURRITO BOWL		QUESIDILLAS					
WHOLE CHICKEN							
MONGOLIAN BEEF							

Meal Brainstorming

Coming up with dinner ideas to plug into my meal plan for the week can sometimes be the longest part of the job. While meal planning itself can be a huge time-saver, I find setting up a simple collection with just lists of ideas can save me time during the actual planning stage itself. How many times have you sat down to meal plan and spent 30 minutes just trying to decide what you like to eat? A collection like this can be set up like mine, by prep times, or you could separate it by main ingredient or even organize it into cuisines such as Mexican, Indian, Chinese, etc. I find it easiest to set up a weekly routine with a loop of some sort and then just plug in what sounds interesting to me (or what I have ingredients for in my fridge).

HOME CARE

Due to the busy nature of my life, my home is the part of my life that most often gets ignored because I simply can't neglect my sanity or my family! Before I discovered planning, my life was a mess. We were lucky to eat a dinner that didn't come out of the freezer, and the house was closed for business as far as company went. But the days and weeks that I actually plan my household tasks are among my most productive. To be honest, I rarely get excited about planning out the monotonous task of my days, but I have never regretted setting aside that time and headspace to do so.

Cleaning Schedule

Organizing my cleaning schedule into daily, weekly, monthly, and yearly tasks helps me make sure I fit it all in, including the stuff that I never seem to have time for, like purging closets, cleaning vents, organizing photos, etc. The next two pages in my planner are set aside for family chores. I use this to refer to when we are setting up a family calendar or when I need everybody to pitch in. Even if you don't use a regular chore chart, identifying tasks that can be done well by different members in your family helps you organize your thoughts and establish routines. You could even do something like this to help you organize your regular cleaning tasks and what you want to assign to a housecleaner.

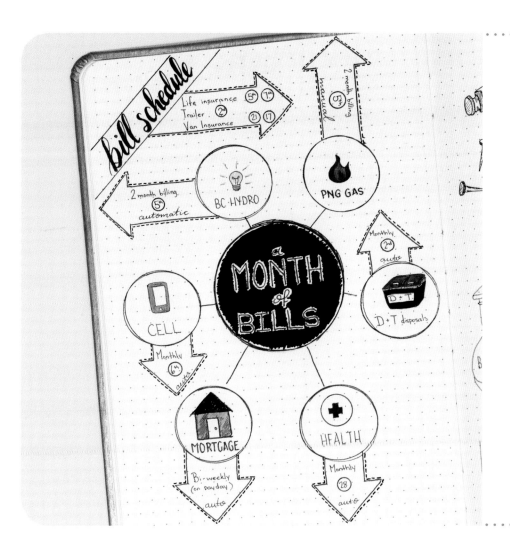

Bill Payments

Online banking can be a real benefit, but I was having trouble keeping track of money flowing in and out of my family's accounts and what was due when. In this collection I simply organized dates that payments are due or scheduled to be made automatically. This way I could adjust our bill payment dates to align better with payday and to make sure I wasn't late on what is to be manually paid. It has been a huge lifesaver!

Home Renos

After purchasing a fixer-upper house, we had a mile-long list of renovations that we wanted to do during our time here. I found that setting up a simple collection of what we wanted to do and the approximate cost of the projects helped us plan when we could tackle the projects, how long they would take, and how much we needed to save.

PERSONAL GROWTH

I like to think of these collections as a sort of vision board for my life. They are the big picture of who I am, and how my plans fit together. They help me remember why I am doing what I am doing, and remind me to take care of myself in the process.

10-Minute Tasks
I am notorious for having so much to do that I can't start anything. I often find myself with just a few minutes between activities and was spending them on social media because it isn't enough time to really get into a large task on my "to-do" list. Setting up a collection of 10-minute tasks gives me an array of things I can accomplish in those small amounts of downtime that are otherwise so easily wasted.

Recharging
Investing in myself tends to be my last priority. Creating a collection of simple, quick things I can do to recharge my batteries has been instrumental in taking better care of myself.

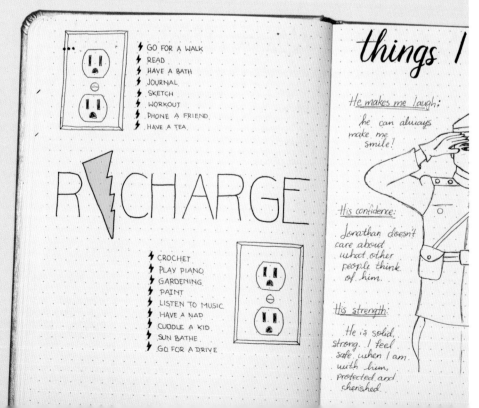

ORNING ROUTINE

- GET READY
- DEVOTIONS
- E-MAILS
- SCHEDULING
- BREAKFAST
- TIDY
- LAUNDRY
- LIVE
- MORNING BASKET
- PLANNING
- SCHOOL with KIDS

MY EVENING ROUTINE

- TIDY the KITCHEN
- MAKE COFFEE
- PREP BREAD
- JANIAH'S BEDTIME
- ALIYAH'S BEDTIME
- OLDER KIDS BED
- TEA and JOURNALING
- BRUSH TEETH
- WASH my FACE
- READ a BOOK
- BED

23

Routines Collection

I wanted to show you how you could use a collection to set up a routine of any kind. A routine is a bit different than a schedule because rather than give specific times to accomplish each task, you simply lay out a general flow to follow. I love how simple this is, and yet it still lends a lot of flexibility and beauty. I find this helpful for my planning routine, starting and ending my day, my school routine with the kids, and even my workout routine!

Goals

Every planner needs to have a goals page. While some people set up a monthly goals page, others choose to do a yearly goals page. I love doing both! I find that I need small, reachable goals that point me towards my big-picture goals and plans. My yearly goal collection is more of a dreaming page that contains the things I hope to achieve that year. I use my monthly pages to organize how I can make those happen in actionable steps.

GOALS

READ 20 books

Home Renos:
- paint
- do floors
- re-do kids' rooms
- kitchen

LEARN to knit!

vacation!

Get chickens & build a garden!

ENTERTAINMENT

We all need to kick back and relax and do something that we love every once in a while. These collections give you some examples of how you can keep track of your ideas so you always have something on hand when you feel like you need to recharge.

Movies to Watch

With so many movie recommendations, setting up a collection like this can help you keep track of what you want to watch, and even help you set aside time to actually watch them. This was a fun, simple collection I did and I plan to color in the popcorn kernels as I watch each show. With my hubby being a big sci-fi fan, I have a feeling it's going to be a long time before I get to all these chick flicks!

Books to Read

This is a tremendously popular collection. It is a visual representation of all the books you plan to read that year/quarter/month. People often color in each spine as the book is read to keep track of what they still want to read. You could even do something like this on one side of the page and use the other side to keep track of library books and their due dates.

Outdoor Fun

Collections are a great way to brainstorm, track, catalog, and even motivate yourself. I love creating lists that get me active, and this spread never ceases to deliver. Whether it's to play a game or do something simple like go for a walk, this gives me lots of reasons to put on my shoes and take in some fresh air. This would also be a great way to track your workouts, your weight loss, your exercise routine, or dog walking!

Packing List

Headed somewhere warm this year? Why not use your planner to organize tasks, contact information, or even what you want to pack? I have a TON of packing collections in my planner; I create a new one for every family vacation or romantic getaway that we do. I can organize it by section and it has saved me from forgetting that phone charger or bathing suit for the umpteenth time!

SERVICE

Investing your time, skills, or money for any cause that is important to you is something worth taking the time to plan. I find that keeping tabs on this area of my life not only helps me be more efficient with my time but also keeps me in check. If you are someone who has trouble saying no, collections such as these can help you set healthy boundaries for yourself and keep you focused on how much you can realistically give of yourself before other areas in your life start to suffer.

Elder Care

I have some friends who are taking care of their aging parents and who asked me to design a collection for them that could be used to help track visits, medications, and other critical information to make this time easier, especially if responsibilities are shared among multiple siblings. This spread shows various medications and instructions, keeps track of important contacts, has a schedule of sibling visiting days and responsibilities, and has an appointment log to keep track of health records.

RX
- zeldonophyl
- moxacil
- benzidopam
- niloxin

INSTRUCTIONS

Zeldonophyl: take on an empty stomach twice a day.
Moxacil: once a day with juice
Benzidopam: as needed
Niloxin: nightly before bed w/ food

Mom's care

IMPORTANT CONTACTS

Family Doctor: Dr. Connors
Office: 250-461-9264

Eye Doctor: Dr. Pinstan
Office: 250-461-6446

Dentist: Dr. Wershaw
Office: 250-461-2269

Specialist: Dr. VanLeid
Office: 250-468-4228

Sara → Mondays: Mom's finances

Colin → Wednesdays: Mom's Groceries

Marie → Fridays: Mom's health

Seth → Sundays: Mom's outings

APPOINTMENTS

DATE	NOTES
04.06.18	dentist appointment - 2 fillings
04.09.18	Dr. Connors upped Moxacil
05.13.18	Eye health exam - schedule surgery
05.19.18	Podiatrist - new compression socks
06.02.18	dentist appointment - cleaning
06.09.18	Echocardiogram - awaiting results
06.30.18	Dr. Connors - referred mom to a cardiologist (Dr. Preston)

My Community

If you are volunteering in any capacity in your local community, a spread like this can help you organize your responsibilities and tasks and evaluate how much time they are taking. This collection can help you decide how many hours you can spend each week in your community, how many volunteer positions you are taking, and whether you are sticking to that in your time log. I find it super helpful to have something like this filled out in pen. Once my three spots are full, it's time to stop putting my hand up at meetings!

Global Causes

Each year our family sends a care package at Christmastime to a child in need. We try to gather various items that we want to share and write letters and draw pictures to give it a personal touch. I have learned over the years that if I don't plan out the things we want to buy or the date it has to be dropped off, we tend to be late or miss it entirely. This year I was determined not to let that happen. This is my collection for global causes. It is a place to help me find and track charities and organizations that I believe in, organize items we are going to donate, and collect food to drop off at the food bank. You could also use a spread like this to track donations to a sponsored child or non-profit organization or even volunteer time at a telethon or relief project, etc.

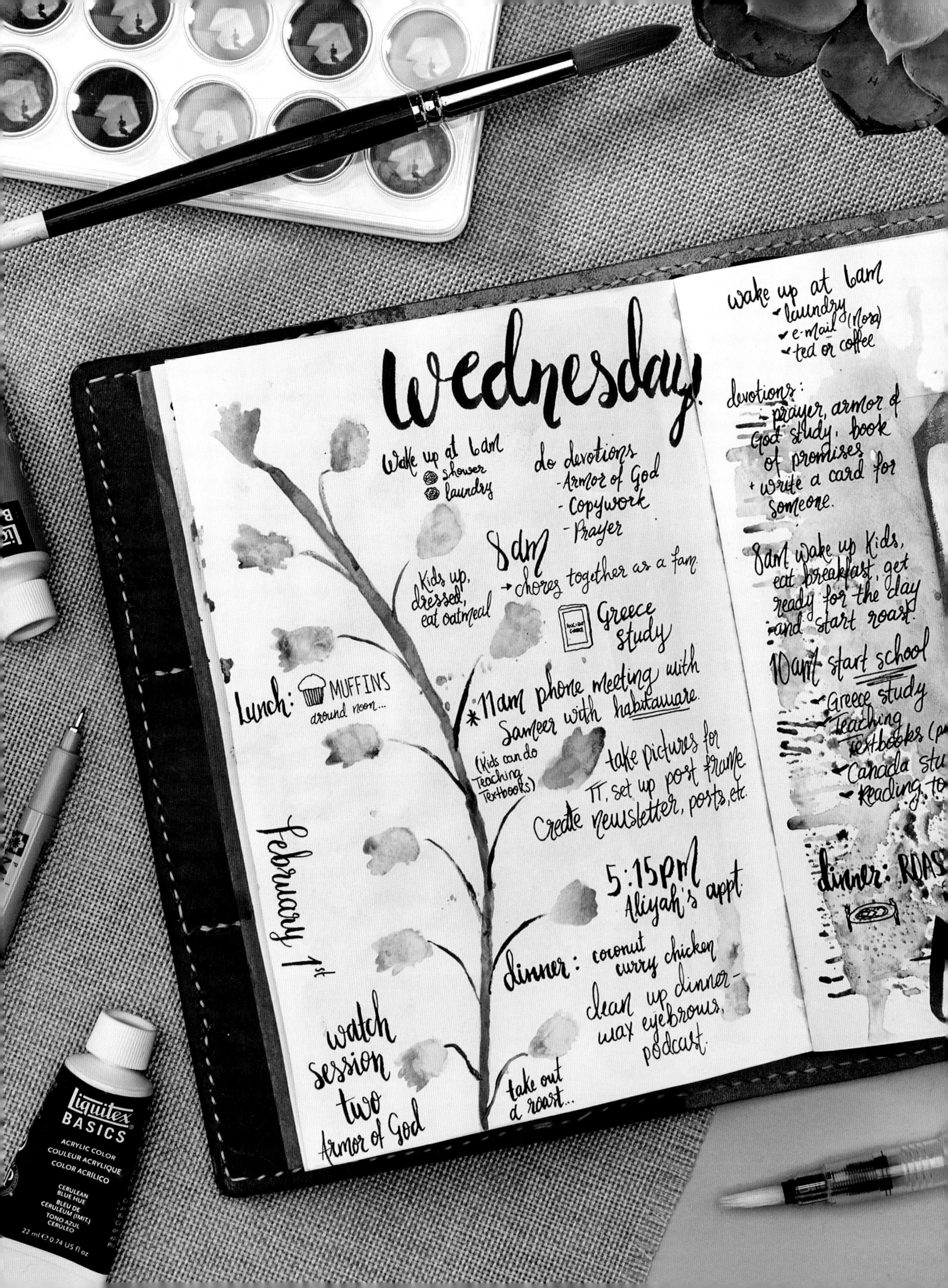

Wednesday

Wake up at 6am
- shower
- laundry

Kids up, dressed, eat oatmeal

do devotions
- Armor of God
- Copywork
- Prayer

8am
→ chores together as a fam.

Greece study

* 11am phone meeting with Sameer with habitaware.

(Kids can do Teaching Textbooks)

Lunch: MUFFINS around noon...

take pictures for FT, set up post frame, create newsletter, posts, etc.

February 1st

5:15pm Aliyah's appt.

dinner: coconut curry chicken

clean up dinner - wax eyebrows, podcast.

take out a roast...

watch session two Armor of God

---

wake up at 6am
- laundry
- e-mail (Nora)
- ted or coffee

devotions:
- prayer, armor of God, study, book of promises
+ write a card for someone.

8am wake up kids, eat breakfast, get ready for the day and start roast.

10am start school
- Greece study
- Teaching textbooks (a)
- Canada stu
- Reading to

dinner: ROAS

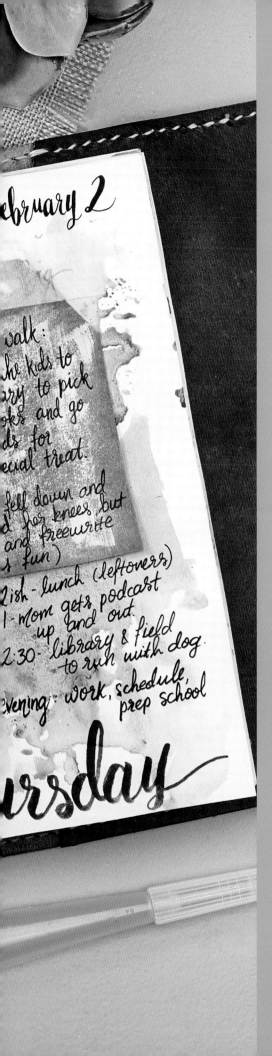

4

STEP BY STEP

• • •

We all love pretty planner pages, but many of us don't feel capable of creating them. I used to think I could never do something like that, that I wasn't artistic, that I didn't have the knowledge or the experience or even the time to make anything beautiful in my planner. However, I have learned that you CAN draw if you take the time to sketch, copy, and study. You CAN paint once you understand the technique. The methods I share in this chapter are all suitable for beginners and are great ways to embellish your planner and make it just a little more "yours." By following these simple steps, you can incorporate these techniques into your planner pages or use the steps as a jumping-off point for something completely different.

Watercolor Ombre

SUPPLIES

wax paper

scissors

your planner

kraft paper and
washi tape to protect
your adjacent page

watercolor paints

water

large watercolor paintbrush

TIME

5–10 minutes
(plus drying time)

DIFFICULTY

easy

PAINTING WITH WATERCOLOR IS ONE OF THE EASIEST

ways to add a splash of creativity and color to your planning pages. I used wax paper to create this ombre effect, but you can use any type of flexible, water-resistant material such as a freezer bag or plastic grocery bag. This is a very forgiving technique that has a beautiful effect you can't get with a paintbrush alone. As you work with this technique, think about which colors inspire you, which colors blend well together, and what they make you think of when you look at them. I have always been attracted to blues and teals; the blend of blue and green is my happy place. With this splattered look, I couldn't help but be reminded of rain as I blended my colors. I decided to make it a collection page with rainy-day activity ideas that I could do with my kids. I added some doodles and whimsical hand lettering to give it a fun, lighthearted feel complete with an optimistic quote at the top.

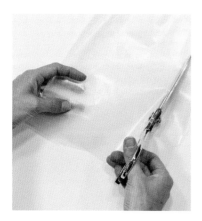

STEP 1 Cut your wax paper to the same size as your journal pages.

STEP 2 Protect the adjacent journal page by taping kraft paper over it. You may also place paper under the page you are working on if you will be using a lot of water.

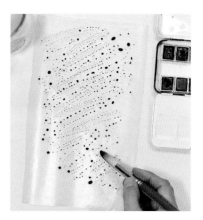

STEP 3 Using one of your colors and lots of water, paint the top of your wax paper. The paint will form dots or small pools. Without rinsing your paintbrush (you want the color to slowly blend), use your second color to paint the bottom portion of your wax paper.

● ● ●

THIS TECHNIQUE can produce a splotchy/splashed look as well as a smooth ombre effect depending on the amount of water you use and how much you smooth the two pages together. Experiment with your technique to find what you like.

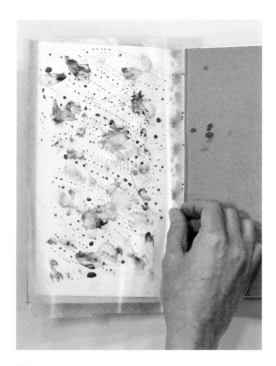

STEP 4 Line up the edges of the wax paper with the edges of your planner and gently lay it painted side down on top of your page.

STEP 5 Gently push and smooth the paper with your fingers to blend the paints.

STEP 6 Holding your planner page flat, slowly peel the wax paper off. Allow the background to dry completely before writing on it.

Layered Acrylic Background

• SUPPLIES

three different colors
(light, dark, and contrast)
acrylic paint

paint palette (or a plate or
piece of plastic to mix your
paints on)

spray bottle

water

paintbrush

drying tool or hair dryer

paper towel

TIME

15 minutes
(plus drying time)

DIFFICULTY

easy

ACRYLIC PAINT GIVES YOUR JOURNAL PAGES A POP

of color that can make your pages truly memorable. I often paint my acrylic backgrounds in batches, pulling out three or four color combinations that I think complement and contrast each other nicely. As I was painting these layers, I kept thinking of the ocean. Because the colors are dark and deep, and I didn't think my black pen would show up on the pages, I decided to mix it up and use a white gel pen to plan our spring trip to the Bahamas. This is one of my favorite spreads; the inspiration really came from the actual process of painting and seeing what ideas, feelings, or thoughts came to my mind as I painted.

STEP 1 Squirt a pea-sized amount of your lightest color of paint onto your palette, then spray it with 8–9 squirts of water to thin. Mix with your paintbrush.

STEP 2 With your paintbrush, spread the diluted paint thinly over your page, changing directions as you paint.

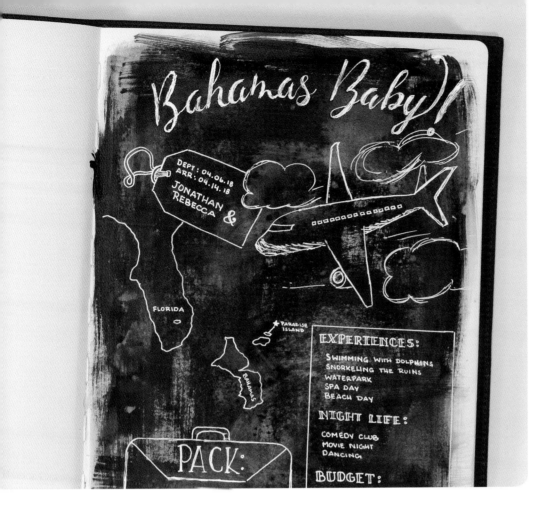

TIP

Don't be afraid to leave white space. You will be layering the paint on and there should be some contrast in the colors.

STEP 3 Let the paint air-dry completely or use a drying tool or hair dryer.

STEP 4 Squirt a dime-sized amount of your dark color. Spray 5–6 times with water and mix with your paintbrush.

STEP 5 With swift, broad strokes, paint your dark color over your light base. Leave some spaces in between and switch directions to add depth to your background.

STEP 6 Spray lightly with water, then dab the surface with a damp paper towel or cloth to lift the paint in some areas. Allow the page to dry completely.

STEP 7 Add your contrasting color to your palate. Dab your paintbrush into the paint, then onto the palette to remove some of the excess so that only a light layer remains.

STEP 8 Lightly paint streaky highlights of your contrasting color over the first two layers until you are satisfied with the amount of color. Don't overdo it!

STEP 9 Spray the page with water and dab to remove paint in selected areas. Allow the page to dry completely before writing on it.

Watercolor Tip In

SUPPLIES

pencil

cardstock or watercolor paper

paintbrush

water

watercolor paints

paper towel

fine marker

washi or double-sided tape or paper clip

TIME

20–25 minutes
(plus drying time)

DIFFICULTY

intermediate

SOMETHING THAT I DO OFTEN IN MY REGULAR PLANNING pages is add a tip in. These are generally a doodle, sketch, drawing, painting, or even a hand-lettered quote that adds a bit of color and fun to my planner without actually taking up room on my pages. All you need for a project like this is a piece of paper that's heavier than you planner pages. Index cards work well, or a small piece of watercolor paper cut to size can be perfect. Just figure out the size you want and pull out your paints! For this project I decided to do a watercolor whale to add to one of my journaling pages. It was relatively simple to make and I love the color that it gives to my finished page.

STEP 1 Sketch your whale shape lightly with pencil onto the cardstock.

STEP 2 With a paintbrush, apply water to a small section of your sketch where you intend to paint your lightest color—in this case, the head of the whale. Dip your paintbrush into your lightest color, then lightly touch the tip to the wet section of your paper, allowing the paint to flow into the water.

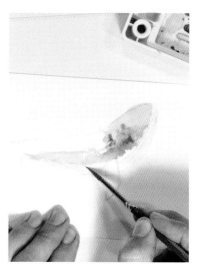

STEP 3 Dip your paintbrush into the next lightest color, and apply that color near the first color in the same area of water. Allow the paints to flow together. Add in your colors one at a time, first wetting your surface with a bit of water and only rinsing your brush when you do not want the colors to blend.

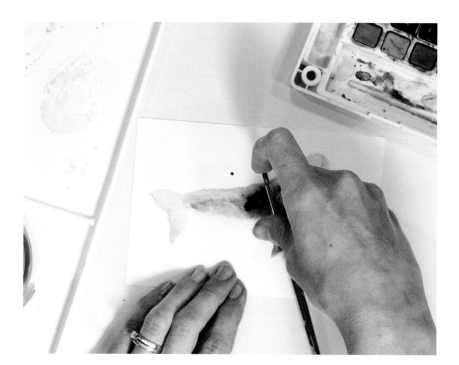

STEP 4 Dip your brush into a darker color. Bend the brush bristles back with your finger and release them to create droplets on your page.

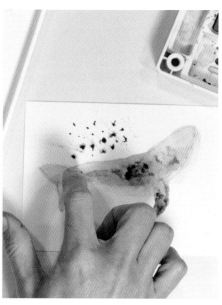

STEP 5 Add water to the body of your whale with your brush. Dip your brush into a contrasting color and apply it just under the whale head. Use your finger to move the paint around.

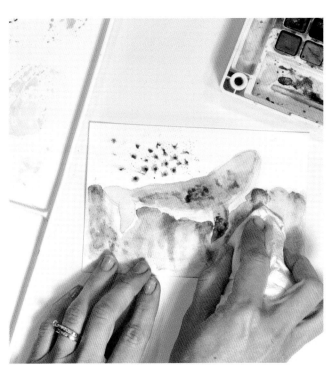

STEP 6 Use a clean, wet brush to create wet streaks under your whale. Add drops of paint to the water and allow them to drip down.

STEP 7 Dab with a damp paper towel or cloth to blend the colors as desired.

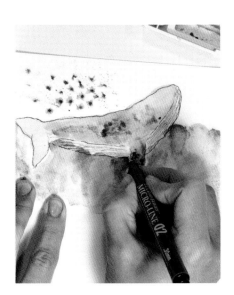

STEP 8 Allow the paint to dry completely, then use a water-resistant black marker to outline the original pencil sketch.

STEP 9 Using washi or double-sided tape on just one side of the tip in or a simple paper clip, secure your artwork or quote in your journal page to create a flap that can be lifted, leaving the page beneath it accessible for writing.

Brush Lettering

SUPPLIES

paper

brush lettering pen

pencil

eraser

TIME

5 minutes

DIFFICULTY

intermediate

I AM A BRUSH LETTERING ADDICT. I LOVE THE RHYTHM of my hands as I move my wrist and push and pull the pen. I love the contrast in the thin lines of the upstrokes and the thick lines of the downstrokes in each letter. To me, brush lettering is the epitome of simple elegance and can dress up a page in just a few minutes. Before you begin working on the technique of brush lettering, note that many things can affect the look of your finished product. There are inexpensive brush lettering pens and expensive ones, supple ones and firm ones. The way you hold your pen, the position of your paper, the slant of your hand, and the type of paper all factor into the result. If you are a perfectionist, play around on scrap paper with different pens, angles, and even shapes of your letters until you find a style you want to use in your planner.

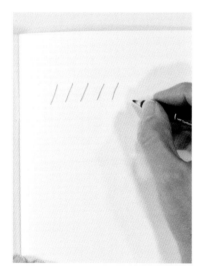

STEP 1 Practice creating thin upstroke lines by holding your pen at a slight angle so that the pen moves upward from left to right. As you create a short line, decrease the pressure of your hand so that the mark is lighter toward the top of the line.

STEP 2 Practice creating thick downstroke lines by holding your pen at the same angle, but moving from top to bottom and keeping constant pressure on the pen.

STEP 3 Before lettering your first word, write it lightly in pencil to take the guesswork out of placement and positioning so you can focus on the up and down movement of your pen.

● ● ●

NOTE

Brush lettering is a bit of an art. It takes practice and some muscle memory to get the technique right. Flip to the back of the book and trace over the brush lettering letters on page 129 to get a better idea of form and style and to practice until you are comfortable if you are feeling stuck.

STEP 4 Go over your pencil lines with your brush pen, decreasing pressure with your upstrokes and pressing down firmly with your downstrokes.

STEP 5 Once your lettering is completely dry, erase your pencil marks.

Cheater Brush Lettering

SUPPLIES

black marker

paper

TIME

5–7 minutes

DIFFICULTY

easy

IF BRUSH LETTERING IS A CHALLENGE FOR YOU BUT you love the look of it, this technique may be perfect for you. It's a simple way to build on your everyday cursive handwriting and turn it into a hand-lettered masterpiece with just a few swipes of your pen. This is the way I began my journal pages. It's not only fast and easy, it's also a great way to train your eye to recognize what brush lettering should look like and to get those gorgeous pages right from the very first day.

STEP 1 Use your pen to write a word of your choice in script.

STEP 2 Draw a parallel line next to each of your downstrokes, angling the second line to smoothly meet the first at the top and bottom of the downstroke.

STEP 3 With your pen, color in the space between your original downstroke and its parallel line, making sure to color only in the same direction as the original lines. You may also do this step using a thicker pen.

Photographic Journaling

SUPPLIES

fallen leaves
journal page
small piece of wax candle
2–3 watercolor paints
water
paintbrush
1–3 photos
photo corners
pencil
black water-resistant marker
eraser
Optional: double-sided tape, washi tape

TIME

20–25 minutes
(plus drying time)

DIFFICULTY

easy

INCLUDING PHOTOS IN YOUR PLANNING, JOURNALING, OR collection pages adds color, personality, and is a great way to keep happy memories close at hand. On this page I decided to do a watercolor resist background to set off some photos, and completed the page with a list of my favorite things about fall. The leaves were so bright outside that I was inspired to use fall colors in my watercolor wash and actual leaves as well. This was a fun spread to put together and has so many elements that make me remember the events of this season.

STEP 1 Arrange your leaves in a pleasing pattern with the veiny underside facing up behind your journaling page.

STEP 2 Holding your candle stub sideways, rub it back and forth over your journaling page, pressing down firmly. Remove the leaves and discard.

STEP 3 Dilute your watercolor paints and paint patches of different colors over the waxed areas.

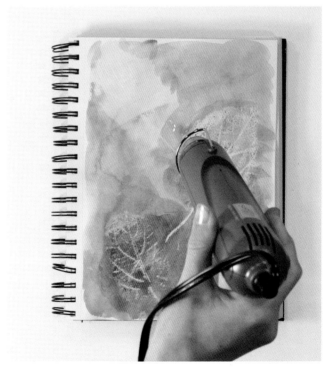

STEP 4 Mix and blend the colors on your page to highlight the veins and outline of the leaves.

STEP 5 Let air-dry completely or use a drying tool.

STEP 6 Arrange your photos over the painted surface and adhere them to the page with photo corners, double-side tape, or washi tape.

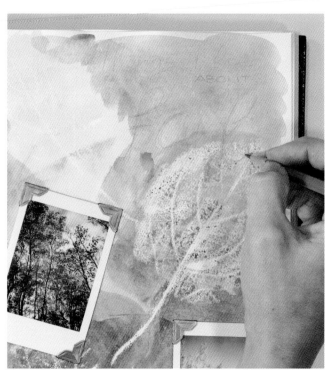

STEP 7 Lightly pencil in your page heading, focusing on placement and design of the lettering.

STEP 8 Go over your pencil lines with your black water-resistant marker or brush marker. Wait a moment or two, then erase any visible pencil lines.

STEP 9 With a black water-resistant marker, add items to your collection. Or, if you prefer, use this page for journaling.

Custom Tabs

ORGANIZING YOUR PLANNER WITH TABS CAN SAVE YOU
time rifling through to find your months, collections, and daily planning lists. You can make your tabs out of paper, though I recommend using a laminator or specialized tab stickers to make them more durable. They do tend to get a bit of rough treatment because they extend over the edge of your pages. Here I'll show you how to make paper tabs using a laminator, and also how to use a tab punch and laminating stickers from your local craft store.

SUPPLIES • · · · · · ·

FOR LAMINATED TABS:
pencil
paper
ruler
scissors
pen
laminating pouches
laminator
washi or
double-sided tape

FOR PUNCHED TABS:
tab punch
decorative paper
pencil
marker or pen
eraser
tab stickers

TIME
8–10 minutes

DIFFICULTY
easy

LAMINATED TABS

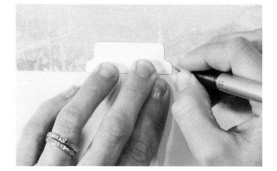

STEP 1 With pencil, trace your tab shapes onto paper using the guide on page 135, or draw your own shape using a ruler. Carefully cut out.

STEP 2 Write the subject onto each tab, then place them into the laminating pouch. I do as many of these at once as I can to make the best use of the pouch.

STEP 3 Run your pouch through your laminator to seal it; cut out the tabs.

STEP 4 Tape your tabs into your journal with either washi tape or double-sided tape, staggering the positions so they are easier to access.

TIP

It you don't have access to a laminator, enclose each tab in a piece of clear packing tape, then cut out. If you leave a portion of the packing tape exposed at the bottom of your tab, you can use this to tape the tab into your planner.

VARIATION Make large tabs for your monthly pages that can serve as a tab and a calendar at the same time. There is a template for this on page 135.

PUNCHED TABS

STEP 1 Using the punch, cut out as many tabs as desired from your decorative paper.

STEP 2 Write the subject on the tab in pencil, then go over decoratively with pen using the cheater brush technique (see page 108) if desired. Erase any visible pencil lines.

STEP 3 Position the written tab onto one side of the sticker and affix to the back of the desired planner page.

STEP 4 Fold your sticker over onto the other side and press firmly to secure.

Corner Bookmark

● SUPPLIES

scrap paper

ruler

scissors

pencil

washi tape

TIME

10 minutes

DIFFICULTY

easy

ASIDE FROM THE CREATIVE ELEMENTS YOU CAN ADD to your planning pages, there are also practical items you can use that will enhance your planning experience. Many of these are very easy to make yourself, rather than purchase. For example, these corner bookmarks are a handy way to mark your place in your planner. They are quick and easy to create, and have myriad uses both in your planner and in other books.

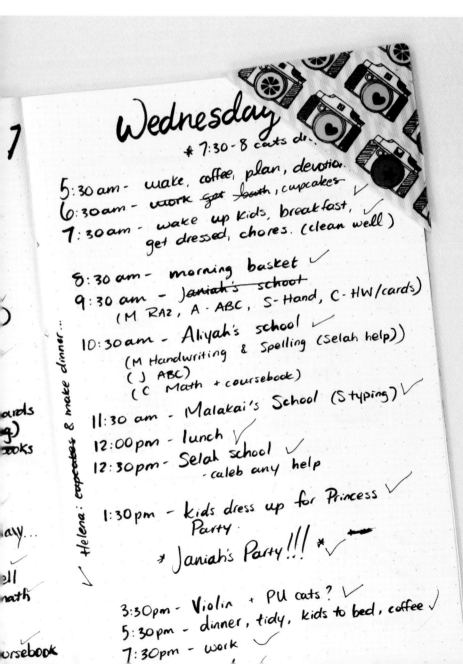

STEP 1 On scrap paper, measure out a 4" x 4" square and cut out.

STEP 2 Fold your square in half, carefully lining up the edges, then reopen to reveal a crease down the middle.

STEP 3 Fold your square again, this time from corner to corner, forming a triangle. Open your square again; there are now two creases that cross in the middle.

STEP 4 Fold one of your corners down to the middle point of the creases. Repeat with the opposite side so that your points touch in the middle.

STEP 5 Fold the paper in half, bringing your folded-down edges together.

STEP 6 Fold in your two outer corners up to the middle and turn so that the longer points are toward your work surface.

STEP 7 Working one at a time, fold each of the two longer points into the middle to form your paper into a triangle.

STEP 8 Cover the triangle with washi tap, making sure to leave an opening along the side opposite the point.

MY STORY

I use corner bookmarks to group different sections. However, the one I use most often is one labeled "today" that I use it to mark my place in my daily section.

Decorative Planner Clip

SUPPLIES

paper, ribbon, or felt
ruler
pencil
scissors
paper clip
double-sided tape

TIME

5 minutes

DIFFICULTY

easy

PLANNER CLIPS ARE POPULAR ACCESSORIES. YOU CAN use them to mark a particular page, or to group collections or sections. I often use a clip to mark my running lists so I can refer to them quickly. There are dozens of different types for sale in stores and on the internet. However, you can easily make your own in any size to accent your journal with some simple scraps of felt, ribbon, scrapbooking paper, and a paper clip. I love making them out of pretty paper that sticks out of my traveler's notebook.

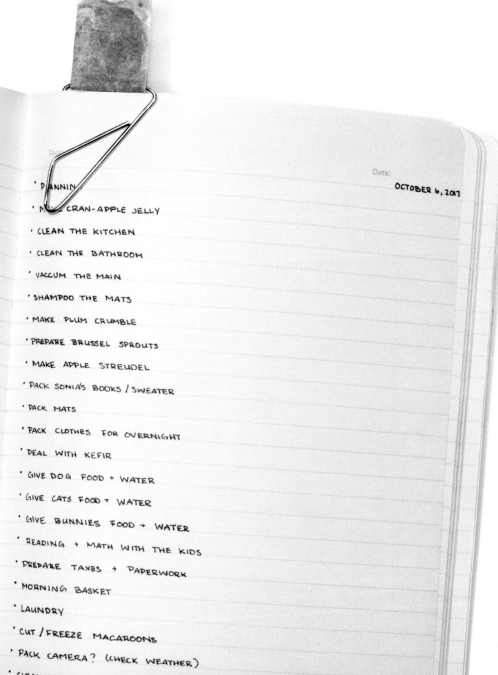

Date:

Tags:

Date:

OCTOBER 6, 2017

- PLANNING
- MAKE CRAN-APPLE JELLY
- CLEAN THE KITCHEN
- CLEAN THE BATHROOM
- VACCUM THE MAIN
- SHAMPOO THE MATS
- MAKE PLUM CRUMBLE
- PREPARE BRUSSEL SPROUTS
- MAKE APPLE STREUDEL
- PACK SONIA'S BOOKS / SWEATER
- PACK MATS
- PACK CLOTHES FOR OVERNIGHT
- DEAL WITH KEFIR
- GIVE DOG FOOD + WATER
- GIVE CATS FOOD + WATER
- GIVE BUNNIES FOOD + WATER
- READING + MATH WITH THE KIDS
- PREPARE TAXES + PAPERWORK
- MORNING BASKET
- LAUNDRY
- CUT / FREEZE MACAROONS
- PACK CAMERA? (CHECK WEATHER)
- CLEAN T

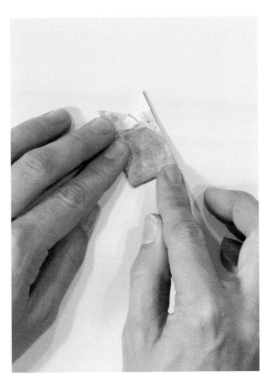

STEP 1 On a piece of paper, draw a rectangle about 1 1/2" wide by 6" tall, with a notch about 1" deep at each end, or use the template on page 135. Cut out.

STEP 2 Fold up the notched edges to meet.

STEP 1 ...or use the template on page 135.

(TIP)

It's even easier to create a clip with ribbon. Simply cut several lengths of ribbon approximately 6" long and tie in a knot around the clip. To create a felt clip, follow the steps at left but use fabric glue to adhere the two sides together.

STEP 3 Insert your folded paper rectangle into the clip.

STEP 4 Place double-sided tape on the inside of your paper and press firmly to secure. Insert paper clip into your planner to mark your desired spot.

Custom Pockets

● SUPPLIES

ruler

your notebook (to measure)

cardstock

pencil

scissors

bone folder

double-sided tape

TIME

10 minutes

DIFFICULTY

easy

I LOVE TO HAVE POCKETS IN MY PLANNER. THE MORE

pockets, the better! I love filling them up with stickers and scrap pieces of paper or tip ins that I have watercolored or sketched that I might want to use, etc. While some journals and notebooks come with a pocket or two, it is really quite easy to make as many as you need in your planner to store anything from receipts to notes. It's a great way to add functionality and beauty to your book.

STEP 1 Determine the final size of your pocket by plotting out different dimensions on a page in your planner. Decide how big you want your pocket to be and write down the measurements. Or, use the template on page 135.

STEP 2 Measure the desired dimensions for your finished pocket onto your cardstock, adding 1/2" to the height of the pocket and 2" to the width. Cut your cardstock to these dimensions.

STEP 3 Make a mark 1" in on each side and 1/2" up from the bottom. Fold the sides in to the marks to form a flap; use a bone folder or other hard object to press the crease firmly.

STEP 4 Fold each flap in half along its length accordion style, so that the wrong side of the paper is facing out. Press the crease firmly.

STEP 5 Fold the bottom 1/2" up to match your line; press firmly along the fold.

STEP 6 Apply double-sided tape along the outer side of all three flaps.

STEP 7 Position your pocket in the desired place on your page and press firmly into place, pressing down for about 10 seconds along the edges to secure.

Make Your Own Notebook

SUPPLIES

heavy cardstock for the cover
(kraft paper or scrapbook
paper work well)

ruler

pencil

scissors

bone folder

paper for text pages

paper cutter

string (I like hemp or waxed
thread)

large sewing needle

Optional: awl

TIME

25–30 minutes

DIFFICULTY

easy

MAKING YOUR OWN NOTEBOOKS IS HANDY SKILL. YOU can create them in any size that works for your style of planning. You can use them as inserts for your traveler's notebook, as your everyday notebook or journal, or as a book to plan a special event. You can use fancy scrapbook paper or simple craft paper for your cover. For your pages, you can use anything from high-end watercolor paper to basic printer paper. It's not only a great way to save some cash, but it also helps you focus on how you will be using your book right from the beginning.

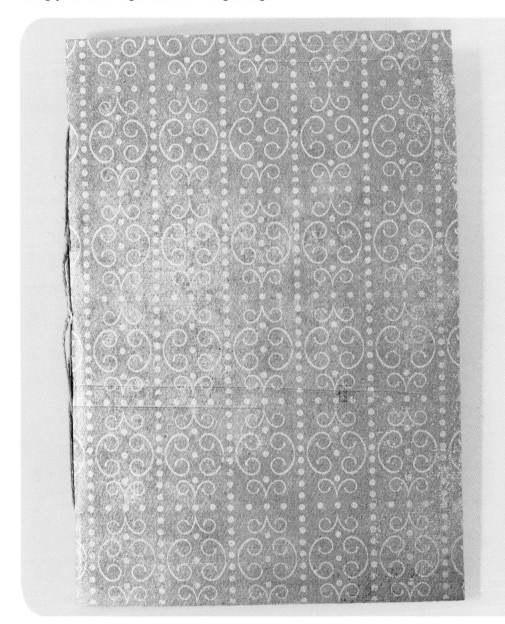

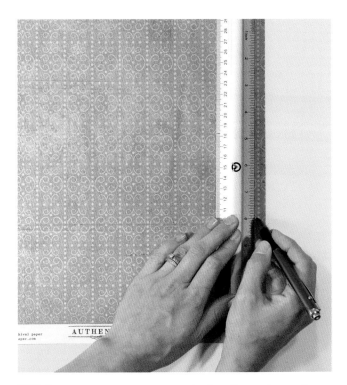

STEP 1 On your cardstock, mark the dimensions of your open book. I've used 8 1/4" tall by 9" wide, which will include about 3/8" for the folded spine.

STEP 2 Cut out your cover.

STEP 3 Fold your cover in half along with width, using a bone folder or ruler to crease your fold.

STEP 4 Mark the dimensions for your text pages on your text paper. I've chosen 8 1/4" long by 8 3/4" wide, which allows for a bit of an overhang of the cover. Cut to the same dimensions as your cover if you want your pages to be flush.

STEP 5 Cut your inside pages with scissors or a paper cutter if you have one.

STEP 6 Fold each page in half separately along the width, and crease the fold of each piece with a bone folder or ruler. Place each folded page into the previous page. Trim the pages evenly if necessary.

STEP 7 Cut a piece of waxed thread or hemp at least 3.5 times the height of your book and thread it through your needle.

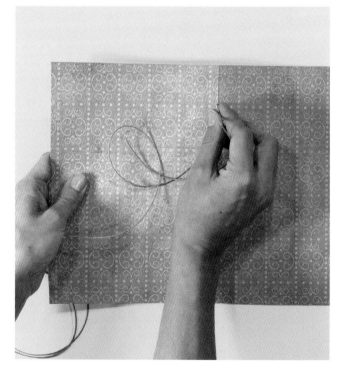

STEP 8 Turning your notebook face down, start a few inches from the top and pierce your needle down through the spine, poking through the cover and all pages. (If you have an awl on hand, it helps to pierce your holes first but it isn't necessary).

STEP 9 Turn over your notebook and pierce your needle back through the middle of the spine.

STEP 10 Come back up with your needle a few inches from the bottom (same distance as from the top). Repeat the process, going back up the spine until each side has two threads.

STEP 11 Go back down the middle of the spine one last time.

STEP 12 Tie your end pieces together on the outside of the cover and trim any excess string.

RESOURCES

Feather Traveler's Notebook: This is from a little Etsy shop called Elrohir Leather. They hand make beautiful, custom traveler's notebooks. You can find them at https://www.etsy.com/shop/elrohirleather.

Passport-Size Yellow Traveler's Notebook: Find this beauty on Etsy at https://www.etsy.com/shop/PohakantenJournals.

Wallet Insert: You can get wallet inserts like this custom made at foxyfix.com. The particular one I had made was the Havasu Terracotta Wallet Insert Couture No. 1 / Design 3 D 1.

Pink Standard Traveler's Notebook: This is one of my favorites. I love the size, it fits perfectly into your hands, it has card slots built right in, and it is excellent quality. You can snag this beauty along with many others at Speckled Fawns at speckledfawns.com.

Lion Traveler's Notebook: This was my first custom-made traveler's notebook. I had this extra-wide size created for my faith journaling at an Etsy shop called Alt Guild. Find it at https://www.etsy.com/shop/altguild.

Inserts: Many of the inserts shown in these pages are handmade. I purchased some of my larger ones from Elrohir Leather (my favorite are her cartridge paper inserts, which hold media very well).

Favorite Notebooks: My top three notebooks right now are from doubleedgednotes.com, Leuchtturm (I usually get those on Amazon), and Rhodia (again, readily accessible on Amazon). These are all high-end notebooks that have beautiful paper and can be used in a wide variety of ways.

Favorite Pens: I am a sucker for pens, but my workhorses are my Tombow Fudenosuke brush pens (find them on Amazon or tombowusa.com) and my Copic (imaginationinternationalinc.com/copic) or Micron (Amazon or your local craft store) in .05, 1, and 2mm size felt markers. I can watercolor over them, they don't bleed, they dry quickly, and they are crisp and clear.

Favorite Watercolors: I love my Koi watercolors. I found them on Amazon and they are affordable and have great colors that blend beautifully! Just make sure you get yourself a decent brush set and you're good to go.

Additional Supplies: If you are looking for photo corners, a heat tool for drying, nice pencil crayons, or any other specialty supplies, you will likely have the most success at a craft or scrapbooking store. Everything from acrylic paint to double-sided tape can be found in those aisles!

Inspiration: There are simply too many gifted journalers and planners to create a comprehensive list. I have found inspiration in a million different sites. Come find me and my social media on my site, rebeccaspooner.com. I handpick my top inspiration each week and post it on Pinterest, Instagram, and more. You can find my links to my favorite people to follow there.

INDEX

Cursive Brush Font

Aa Bb Cc Dd
Ee Ff Gg Hh
Ii Jj Kk Ll
Mm Nn Oo Pp
Qq Rr Ss Tt
Uu Vv Ww Xx
Yy Zz

BLOCK LETTERING

Aa Bb Cc Dd

Ee Ff Gg Hh

Ii Jj Kk Ll

Mm Nn Oo Pp

Qq Rr Ss Tt

Uu Vv Ww Xx

Yy Zz

BOLD BLOCK LETTERING

Aa Bb Cc Dd Ee

Ff Gg Hh Ii Jj

Kk Ll Mm Nn Oo

Pp Qq Rr Ss Tt

Uu Vv Ww Xx Yy

Zz

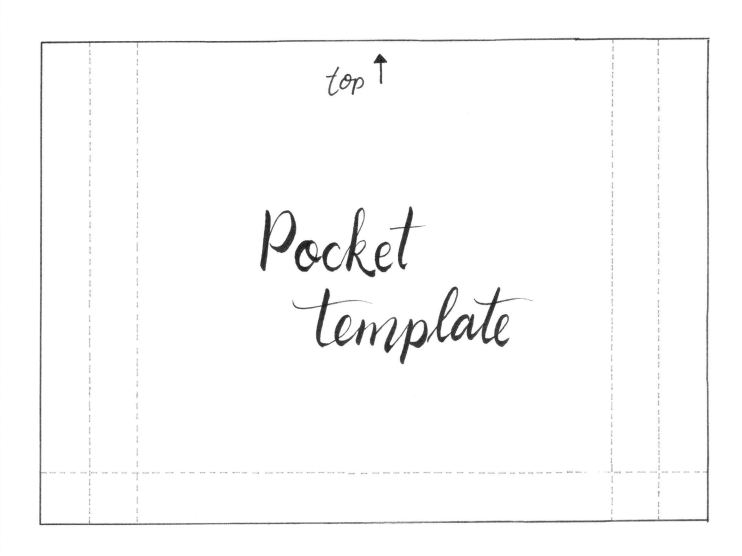

top ↑

Pocket template

Monthly tab template

paperclip template

tab template

Animal Doodles

dividers

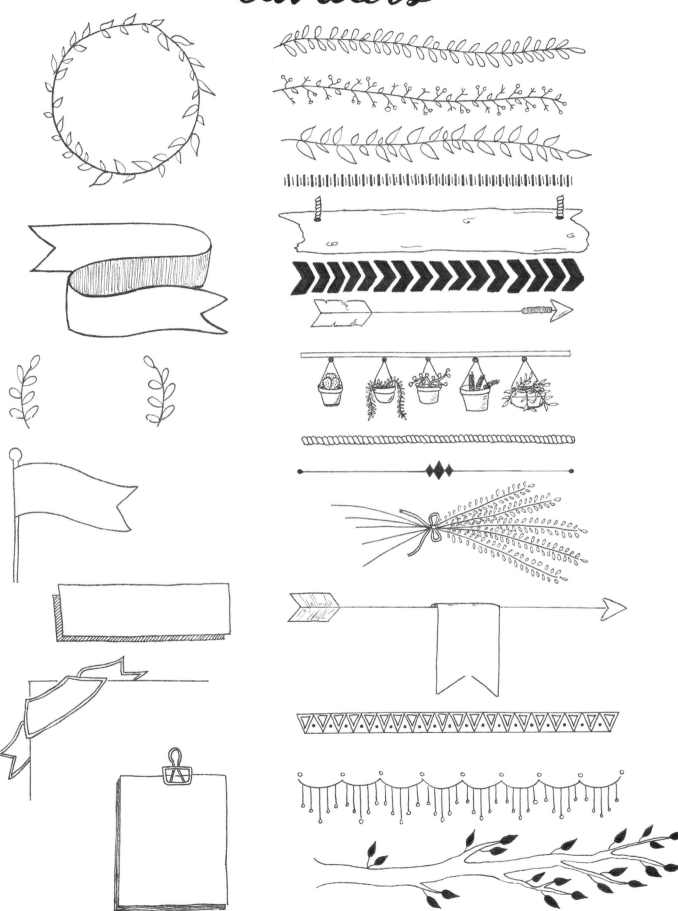

flowers AND wreaths

Planner Doodles